Entertaining Celebrations

Celebrate Each Month with Pizzazz!

by

Beverly Reese Church

with

Sallye English Irvine

Photographs by Tina Freeman

Design by Kristin Peterson O'Loughlin

*Illustrations by Elizabeth Pipes Swanson
and Luis Colmenares*

Contents

Contents

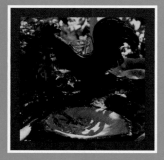

* Indicates
recipe is given
on pages
70-92

† Indicates item
is available for
sale on page 94

January

Fabulous flower strewn tulle adds drama draped over chairs and table.

A Pasta Party with "Pastabilities"

For many, January is a cold and quiet month. The glittering holiday whirl has settled to a surprisingly silent calm. The decorations are down and snugly packed away. We're paying bills and trying to keep those New Year's resolutions. All the excitement appears to be over - at least for the time being. So midway into January, let's face it, we're ready for some fun. It's the ideal occasion for a pasta party loaded with pizzazz - the perfect pick-me-up for a mid-winter evening.

The kitchen is brimming with everything guests need to create pasta dishes for everyone to sample. Creativity is the key and "casual chic" is the dress because, after all, we're cookin'!

Here's how it works

Invite four couples - your most fun and theatrical friends. (Call in advance so you can put together the perfect guest list.) Then, a week prior to the party, hand-deliver invitations. Guests will be thinking about your party all week long - and honing their pasta cooking skills.

Upon arrival each guest receives a festive, hand-painted apron to don as required party attire. Wine and salad are served - then it's time to pick partners. Have the women (or the men) draw names of the opposite sex and numbers from a funky, fabulous hat or a decorative bowl. The name selected is their partner for the evening. (Anyone picking the name of the person they came with should draw again.) The number indicates the order in which each "couple" will, in turn, head to the kitchen to create a "mini" course of pasta for the rest of the crowd.

Some pasta sauces are already prepared, and an array of optional add-in ingredients like roasted chicken or duck, mussels, shrimp, etc., is waiting. (See recipes from Bacco Restaurant, p. 70, to see which sauces you'll need to prepare ahead.) Presentation is the key, so be sure to stock edible flowers, fresh herbs, strawberries and more.

Each cooking duo, in turn, serves their course to the other guests. Encourage everyone to name their dish. For extra fun, try dancing between courses to give each "couple" time to create and cook.

The invitation – pasta in a box wrapped in a Ray Cole scarf. Handpainted, personalized apron and leaf place mats by Ray Cole.

An antique sideboard illuminated with masses of votive candles.

Napkin petticoats add a whimsical touch to the table.

Wine glasses are tied with Gerbera daisies and galax leaves.

Invitations

Hand-deliver a great box or jar filled with colorful, interestingly shaped pasta. Tie with ribbon and attach a card detailing the party specifics. (You may want to ask each couple to bring their favorite bottle of Italian wine.)

Vegetable centerpiece in the moss-laden flat.

Decorations

Swath the table (we've done the chairs as well) in tulle dotted with fabulous, silk flowers. Craft a dramatic centerpiece of blooms surrounded by traditional Italian ingredients including fresh herbs, eggplant, onions, garlic, tomatoes and red, yellow and green peppers. Napkin petticoats make whimsical place cards. Wine glasses are tied with galax leaves and flowers. Add dozens of flickering votive candles to help set the mood for a magical evening.

Helpful Hints

* This party works best for 10 people, but no more than 12.
* Be sure to keep two large pots of water boiling all the time so the selected pasta can be cooked in a jiffy.
* It's great to have someone helping in the kitchen to keep water boiling and plates and cookware clean - but even if you have help, the "couples" do the serving.
* If you don't have help, consider having the couples that are not in the midst of cooking assist with rinsing and drying plates. However, if you have enough plates for everyone to have a fresh plate for each course, all the better. (Note: The plates need not all be the same pattern, it's often more interesting when they're not.)
* To liven up the party, put five pieces of uncooked, bowtie pasta at each plate. Rate each dish - five bowties being the best. (Remember this is all in fun - most polite people will be merciful in their judging.)

Sumptuous ingredients await the guests creative culinary efforts.

Menu

Chardonnay
Mixed green salad with roasted pecans
Shrimp with Penne Pasta *
Roasted Chicken with Pesto Cream *

Red Zinfandel
Duck Raviolis with Shiitake Mushrooms *

Fume Blanc
Mussels and Linguine *

White Chocolate Lasagna
menu by Bacco Restaurant

* Draw names for dance partners between each course.
* The key to getting people to dance is to play music the group remembers from their high school and college years.
* Music Suggestions: Have an accordion or piano player, or Dean Martin tapes, c.d.'s or any rock n' roll favorites.

Valentine's Day is coming, so it's a great time to celebrate by getting together the day before with "the girls." (If you're like me, you sometimes forget the "big day" - this party is the perfect solution!) During this pre-Valentine's luncheon and "workday" you and your friends can create cards, flower arrangements and other goodies for a dazzling dinner á deux to be staged the following evening. It's a grand way to spend some fun time with friends while everyone ends up indulging their special Valentine.

Here's how it works

On February 1st, call and invite five friends for a "girl's only" luncheon to be held the day before Valentine's Day. The purpose of the party, along with visiting and dining, is to make all the necessary preparations for a romantic dinner with that special someone on Valentine's Day. Ask each guest to bring a large basket, flower clippers, scissors and a fabulous container. (The container will be used for a take-home flower arrangement.) Be sure everyone calls their respective sweethearts to reserve

A rustic basket brimming with everything necessary for a perfect Valentine's celebration.

A Valentine's Feast - a heart-shaped filet and fresh bundle of asparagus atop a heart-shaped, galax-covered charger.

8

February

Pretty pansy
plates cap
heart-shaped,
leaf-covered
chargers.

A bevy of creative items for crafting Valentine's cards on the card-making table.

An ideal one-stop flower arranging location complete with roses, gardenias, verbena and greenery.

Valentine's evening for special plans.

In the morning, before guests arrive, set up several work stations. You will need separate areas for card-making, flower-arranging, and food preparation. (You *could* ask a friend to be responsible for each station.) When all the friends have gathered, serve a quick, light meal. Explain the order in which everything will be prepared during the brief lunch. Then start the activities. As each activity is completed, the finished products are tucked into the baskets. At the end of all the festivities everyone's basket is brimming with all the essential Valentine goodies.

To make Valentine's Day extra special you could consider serving breakfast in bed - with your handmade card on the tray. As evening approaches set the table, chill the champagne and take care of the final touches. Then you will be relaxed and ready for your romantic rendezvous.

Invitation

Call friends on the phone. If you have the time and really want to send an invite, try tucking Valentine treats such as red hots, chocolate kisses and candy hearts inside a pink or red bag. Be sure to include all the party details plus a brief description of purpose of the event - which is to create the perfect Valentine's celebration.

Decorations

For the ladies preparation party, the decor should be simple, perhaps just a few strategically placed pots of red tulips. (Ideally, these can be purchased at the grocery store while shopping for the party necessities.)

Then for the big event, a diminutive table for two, laden with full-blown, perfumed roses, is set for romance. Antique silver glimmers amongst the blooms. Pretty china pieces are offset by the dense, glossy, galax-covered heart chargers. The chairs are cloaked in fabulous, filmy, flower-strewn tulle and each is finished off with a sensational, red satin bow. If you find you are stretched for time, cover the table with a red or floral sheet or tablecloth, then add flowers and a profusion of votive candles. Use the chargers and your best china, flatware and crystal along with your two favorite chairs

Helpful Hints

* Start your party at about 11:00 a.m. so you will have time to eat and complete the Valentine's preparations. Begin right away because most people have busy schedules and you won't want the party to last more than 1½ to 2 hours.
* For the budget-minded, you may want to ask your guests to bring their filets and flowers from their gardens instead of you providing them. Use your own garden to supply as much of the greenery and flowers as possible.
* Save all the trimmings. Freeze the filet trimmings for making chili. Bread trimmings can be used for croutons, for bread pudding or for feeding birds and ducks. Brownie trimmings make marvelous ice cream topping.
* Suggest that your guests bring fairly small containers for their flower arrangements - this is supposed to be quick and easy. (Silver or china pitchers, sugar bowls or creamers make some terrific choices.)
* You can use the red tulle tablecloth and/or chair covers from January's party for the chair covers. Drape over the chairs and tie with a glamorous, red ribbon and bow.

A romantic table set for your special Valentine.

* Be sure to prepare the heart-shaped crostini early in the activity process, as the bread needs to bake for about an hour.
* Music Suggestions: Johnny Mathis, Julio Iglesias or Peggy Lee tapes or CDs - or any other selections you and your "beau" find romantic.

Dinner á Deux Menu

Champagne
Oysters Rockefeller *

Asparagus Bundles tied with Green Onion Strips garnished with Red Pepper Hearts

Heart-Shaped Pasta with Pesto

Heart-Shaped Filet Mignon with Crawfish Etouffée *

Marbleized Mississippi Mud with Hot Fudge Sauce *

menu by Bev Church

March

A favorite red boot makes a marvelous centerpiece when capped with curly willow branches and festive flowers. Courses are served in black skillets tied with napkins.

Spice up the month of March with a Southwestern-style fiesta. Surprise friends by staging this party at an eclectic art gallery or studio where white-washed walls punctuated with splashes of colorful, creative art set the tone for a sizzling soirée.

Host this party with several couples or barter with a friend that has a gallery. The evening can include interacting with the artists as well as dining and dancing. It's a sensational celebration, especially after several stark months of chilly winter weather.

Here's how it works

Invite up to 50 friends for a casual night of dining, dancing and action. Guests should arrive clad in cowboy boots and jeans or other appropriate casual fiesta attire. Music, featuring a Mariachi band, classical guitar or favorite country and western tunes fills the air. Cold south-of-the-border brands of beers and icy margaritas are served as guests stroll about viewing the art on display and talking to the artists. Dinner is served buffet-style and guests are seated at tables dotted throughout the gallery.

Southwestern-Style Fiesta in an Art Gallery

A ribbon-tied Tabasco® bottle makes a "hot" hand-delivered invite or place card.

An eclectic art gallery or studio makes the perfect backdrop for wild, imaginative decor and festive individual table designs.

13

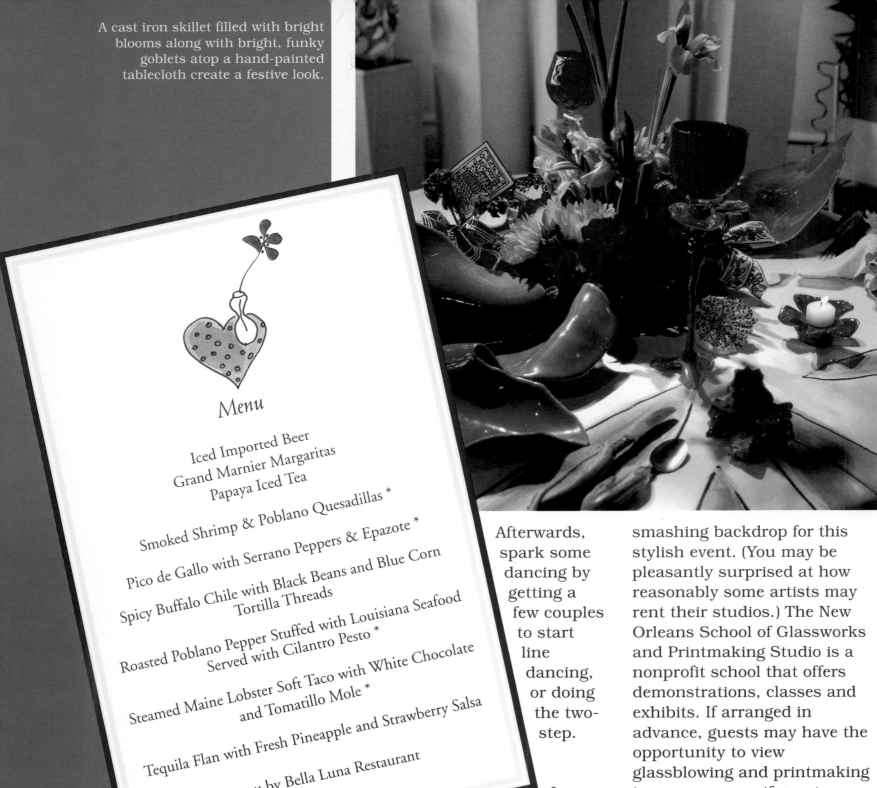

Menu

Iced Imported Beer
Grand Marnier Margaritas
Papaya Iced Tea

Smoked Shrimp & Poblano Quesadillas *

Pico de Gallo with Serrano Peppers & Epazote *

Spicy Buffalo Chile with Black Beans and Blue Corn
Tortilla Threads

Roasted Poblano Pepper Stuffed with Louisiana Seafood
Served with Cilantro Pesto *

Steamed Maine Lobster Soft Taco with White Chocolate
and Tomatillo Mole *

Tequila Flan with Fresh Pineapple and Strawberry Salsa

menu by Bella Luna Restaurant

Afterwards, spark some dancing by getting a few couples to start line dancing, or doing the two-step.

In most cities there are often dozens of intriguing galleries and studios that could make a smashing backdrop for this stylish event. (You may be pleasantly surprised at how reasonably some artists may rent their studios.) The New Orleans School of Glassworks and Printmaking Studio is a nonprofit school that offers demonstrations, classes and exhibits. If arranged in advance, guests may have the opportunity to view glassblowing and printmaking in progress - or, if guests are feeling especially artistic, they may even be invited to try their hand at either art or possibly print T-shirts to take home.

Invitation

Hand-deliver hot sauce bottles tied with ribbon and a card detailing the party specifics. For alternate ideas try delivering pint-sized jars of homemade pepper jelly tied with raffia, or use small individual cactus plants, with a card attached.

Decorations

Bright blasts of vibrant color energize this spirited evening. Each table boasts its own individual identity: a boot centerpiece is the focal point on one, a skillet centerpiece on another and so forth. Different cloths on each table help keep the look fresh, funky and fun. Galvanized tin containers are filled with curly willow festooned with big, bright paper flowers.

Helpful Hints

* If possible, have each host couple cook a course, or consider having this party catered. We asked Bella Luna.
* Rent a Margarita machine.
* Use CDs and tapes for piped-in music, have a live band or rent a juke box.
* Be sure there is an area with enough floor space for some serious dancing - and try to have someone demonstrate the two-step and some of the latest line-dancing steps.

* Jimmy Maxwell's Music Suggestions: Crazy, On the Road Again, All My Rowdy Friends are Comin' Over Tonight, Boot Scootin' Boogie, Stand by Your Man, Rocky Top, I've Got Friends in Low Places, For the Good Times, Margaritaville, Elvira, Tulsa Time, Blue Eyes Cryin' in the Rain, Stand by Me, La Bamba, I Fall to Pieces, In the Still of the Night, The Way You Do That Thing You Do, Heat Wave, Besame Mucho, Please Release Me.

Canvas-leaf place mats and sunflower napkin rings make fun finishing touches.

Southwest-inspired table cards.

Jazzy Courtyard Brunch

Aspidistra leaf stirrers

Guests can help themselves to champagne and specialty cocktails.

Celebrate the arrival of spring with a decadent jazz brunch. The deliciously balmy air and profusion of blooming, fragrant flowers make this the ideal occasion for entertaining outdoors. Dapper guests dress to the nines - gentlemen sport white linen or seersucker suits, ladies wear their most fabulous hats. A cool, sun dappled courtyard or patio provides the perfect place to while away the afternoon.

Here's how it works

Invite 16 to 20 guests for a relaxed, leisurely weekend brunch. (We chose the shady French Quarter courtyard of Patrick Dunne's Lucullus Antiques in New Orleans, but the party works well on any patio or porch, or in any courtyard or garden.)

To set the mood, hire a small jazz combo or pipe in your favorite tunes. Set up several intimate, bistro tables. Provide decks of cards and an assortment of other games including checkers, chess and backgammon. You could surprise guests by having a few actors from a local theatre group or university come to act out vignettes from Tennessee Williams plays or hire a barbershop quartet.

April

Table set with boxwood-covered container nestled among majolica plates, French stemware and linen napkins.

17

Between courses in the courtyard

Menu

Brennan's Brandy Milk Punch *
Mimosas *
Ramos Gin Fizz *
Chardonnay

Oyster Soup Brennan *
Grillades and Plantation Grits *
Garlic Bread and Cinnamon Toast *
Bananas Foster *

menu by Brennan's Restaurant

Serve classic cocktails - milk punch, mimosas, etc. - in silver pitchers at strategically placed stations around the perimeter of the patio. Enjoy the luxury of an elegant, unhurried afternoon.

Invitation

Inscribe the party specifics on a glossy green aspidistra leaf in gold pen and tie the leaf with a big, beautiful bow. Hand-deliver the bow-bedecked invitation along with a cassette of fabulous jazz music.

Decorations

Petite boxwood planters filled with hydrangeas look stunning without overwhelming small tables. Metal or wooden bistro-style chairs get an extra touch of gaiety when tied with chair back bouquets that double as take-home favors. Minimal additional decoration is needed, the glorious spring weather should suffice - but be sure to showcase any blooming plants (Group them to achieve dramatic impact and buy some extras if you need more color.)

Helpful Hints

* Keep the music soft enough so that comfortable conversation can take place.
* Some people will probably want to dance so save a little space on the patio for that purpose.
* If you don't have, and can't rent or borrow ice cream parlor-style tables and chairs, use card tables draped with attractive fabric or sheets.
* If the sun is strong where you're holding the party, use market umbrellas.
* If the weather really warms up, encourage the men to take their jackets off.

* Jimmy Maxwell's Music Suggestions:
Way Down Yonder in New Orleans, Up the Lazy River, Exactly Like You, Beal Street Blues, Bourbon Street Parade, Hello Dolly, Just a Closer Walk With Thee, Basin Street Blues, Muskrat Ramble, Twelfth Street Rag, Yellow Dog Blues, Alexander's Ragtime Band, The Entertainer, Doctor Jazz, Ain't She Sweet, Is It True What They Say About Dixie, Ain't Gonna Give You None of My Jelly Roll, Night Train.

Buffet table is laden with Brennan's Grillades and Grits in the courtyard.

Sun drenched courtyard with bistro tables and antique iron chairs with chair back bouquets.

19

Table spread with a quilt has handpainted napkins and a stenciled apron for each guest.

Napkin rings are tiny watering cans filled with flowers.

*M*ay is the perfect month for a garden party. Nature is ablaze with vibrant color. Verdant foliage is everywhere along with a stunning palette of blooms in lilac, fuschia, fiery red and other spectacular shades. The weather is sheer perfection and the intoxicating perfume of roses wafts through the gentle, stirring breeze. There's perhaps no better time to celebrate the splendor of spring - so dine al fresco with your gardening friends.

Here's how it works

This outdoor event is perfect for your garden club friends or any others who share a passion for the garden. Invite approximately six to twelve guests of all ages - gardening is the common denominator.

An 11:30 a.m. arrival time works well. Set tables amid blooming areas and flowered walkways. (We chose the New Orleans Botanical Gardens in City Park, but any attractive garden makes a suitable setting.)

Request that each guest write down, and bring along, a gardening tip to share with the group and perhaps some gardening books to

May

N.K. LAWN & GARDEN CO.
SENSATION MIX
COSMOS

Hand-delivered
invitation is a leafy
cabbage with flowers,
seed packets and
party information.

21

Silk flower pen and pad

recommend along with any cuttings from favorite or unusual heirloom plants. Upon arrival, ask guests to put their gardening tips in a basket. (See helpful hints for examples of gardening tips.) Offer drinks and the crabmeat appetizer, then encourage guests to stroll about the garden. Serve lunch. After everyone has finished their scrumptious strawberry shortcake, read the gardening tips aloud. (Decorated notepads, which double as place cards, provide a place for jotting down the useful information.) Then share any cuttings, along with other tried and true gardening advice. Guests go home with a hand-stenciled gardening apron complete with gloves, seed packets and other garden-inspired goodies.

Invitation

Hand-deliver a leafy cabbage adorned with flowers in a terracotta saucer. Surround the cabbage with seed packets and a card detailing the party information.

Decorations

A spring garden doesn't need much decoration, but for added effect try topping tables with trellises entwined with ivy, flowers and other greenery. Use antique quilts in lieu of tablecloths for a classic, traditional touch. Finish off folding chairs with fabulous ribbon and a coat of basil paint. Clay saucers crowned with cabbage leaves serve as clever chargers. Bloom bedecked pens and pads make marvelous place cards and take home favors.

Trellis centerpiece

Helpful Hints

* If you hold the event in a Botanical Garden, brush up on horticultural and historical information so that you can help answer any questions that might arise (or if possible, engage a docent).
* If the party is in a private garden, have guests bring clippers and share cuttings with them. Be sure to provide plastic cups or small zip-lock style bags for transporting the cuttings.
* If time allows, consider playing bridge or cards after the luncheon.
* If you can't find a terrific trellis, make your own out of bamboo tied with raffia to look like a windowpane.
* Example of a gardening tip: To get rid of snails, put a small cup filled with beer in the flower bed. The snails, which are attracted to the beer, get trapped in the cup. Dispose of them in the most humane way possible. Too bad they can't be escargot!
* Music Suggestions: Classic symphony such as Vivaldi, Mozart or Debussy on a boombox.

Tables are also set in the greenhouse amid rare orchids. A tapestry is spread on the table with cabbage leaf service plates.

Menu

Chilled Chardonnay
Mimosas
Strawberry Pear Cocktails *

Crabmeat Salad on French Bread
Croutons *

Soft Shell Crabs with Almonds and
Shallot Dill Vinaigrette *

Strawberry Shortcake *

menu by Mr. B's Bistro

Set Sail on the High Seas

Colorful Chinese carton invitations ready for delivery.

All is ready for guests to set sail.

Sunflower rimmed baskets and colorful Chinese cartons make a cheery and delightfully portable way to serve a cold supper on the boat or beach.

*J*une is the dawn of summer - a month of soothing warm breezes, sparkling sand and brilliant, silvery, sun-illuminated waves. It's that splendid time of year, action-packed with outdoor activities, when most people find themselves irresistibly drawn to the water. So head to the lake, the beach or the bay for swimming, sailing, splashing and simply soaking up the glorious, golden sunshine. And be sure to celebrate the season with a sunset cruise and a memorable meal.

Here's how it works

Have guests arrive at an appointed place: the local yacht club, marina or pier. Bring along a cassette or CD player so the air will be filled with summery, beach-inspired tunes. Serve icy cocktails in silver julep cups and socialize while you wait for your group to gather. When the gang's all there, rev the engines or set sail for a fun destination, preferably a spot with a beach. To make the potables and other party goodies portable, stash them safely inside individual, decorated beach bags - each couple gets a tote.

June

Flags festoon the boat and flutter in the breeze while underneath a "moveable feast" and an inviting tray of icy cold cocktails await guests.

25

Bouquet-tied beach totes are brimming with crusty baguettes and other goodies in preparation for supper on the shore.

After arriving at a suitable spot, arrange blankets or beach towels and let the fun begin. Start the music and serve a cold supper out of bright-colored Chinese cartons and sunflower baskets. Sit back and watch the sunset then cruise back to the home port before it gets too dark.

Invitations

Hand-deliver colorful Chinese cartons filled with fun, crinkly paper and theme-appropriate items such as seashells, sand dollars, toy sailboats, etc. Write the party information on palm trees and fish fashioned out of mylar and add these to the cartons. For another invitation idea, consider purchasing inexpensive yachting flags and writing the party details on the flags with a black laundry marker.

Decorations

Fun flags, windsocks and other fluttering decorations add to the atmosphere on-board. Beach umbrellas and big towels are all that are needed ashore. Let the sunset do the rest.

Helpful Hints

* Try to begin the festivities around 3:30 or 4:00 in the afternoon. That way you'll avoid the burning heat.
* Encourage guests to wear a bathing suit under their clothing. Everyone should also bring along sunscreen and hats, and be sure to remind guests to wear shoes that they won't mind getting wet (it's almost impossible to get a boat all the way up on shore).
* Don't forget extra towels.
* When you arrive at your destination, hold a sand castle building competition, look for seashells or take a scenic stroll. You could also arrange to set up badminton or volleyball.
* Music Suggestions: Beach favorites by such artists as Jimmy Buffett, Bob Marley and the Wailers, the Beach Boys or tunes with a Caribbean beat.

More creative invitation ideas.

A duo of umbrellas cast a spot of shade on the sunny shore.

menu

Veuve Clicquot Champagne
Galatoire's Special Cocktails

Shrimp Remoulade *
Potatoes Brabant
Crawfish Salad *
Godchaux Salad *

Crepes Maison with Triple Sec *

menu by Galatoire's

27

July

Old-Fashioned Family Picnic

Family parties are always "the best"! Nothing is more fun than having all ages together from babies to grandparents. Bare feet in the cool green grass, children's laughter radiating in the warm sunshine and icy, wet watermelon - these are just a few of the glories of the season. It's a time for togetherness and for frolicking outdoors - so celebrate summertime with a classic, old-fashioned, family picnic complete with all the trimmings.

Here's how it works

Invite a dozen or more families for an old-fashioned picnic (Plan for about 60-75 guests in all). This party works best when held in a large open space. We chose lush, Afton Villa in St. Francisville, Louisiana, but you could plan this event in almost any country location or park.

Encourage any guests with musical talent to bring along their instruments (guitar, fiddle, ukulele, harmonica, accordion, etc.) to play at the picnic. As guests arrive offer refreshments - soft drinks, beer and minted ice tea for the adults and freshly squeezed lemonade. Then let the games begin. The afternoon activities

The garden invitation - a saucer of potted plants in a riot of summer color, all tied with a snappy, yellow checked bow.

A hand-painted jewelry box makes a whimsical centerpiece with blooms overflowing from the drawers.

29

An umbrella hand-painted with hydrangeas shades the lemonade table.

Agapanthus, allium gargantuan, hydrangea and pink peonies cap a fabric wrapped vase.

should feature a whole host of favorite, outdoor diversions including croquet, three-legged relay races, Red Rover, horseshoes and perhaps even pony rides. Set up a special spot for the children where they can play act, draw pictures, play with dolls and stuffed animals and even make nosegays for Mommy or Grandmother. Serve lunch in the shade, then continue with the amusements. Finish the day's events with music, hand-cranked ice cream, a watermelon seed spitting contest and prizes.

Invitation

Hand-deliver a miniature garden to each family. Place blooming bedding plants in a terracotta saucer, tuck in a pretty card with the party details and finish off with a big, bright bow. (Be sure to let everyone know it's a family affair.)

Decorations

Make a beautiful border to define the picnic area by dotting the grounds with festive torcheres crowned with showy summer blooms. Use cheery color combinations of fabric, such as sunny yellow and azure blue, for a fresh and lively look. Set up several different areas for the fun, including a shady spot with a quilt or canvas rug, surrounded by toys for the tots. Delightful touches that add pizzazz include floral arrangements bursting out of unexpected places - torcheres, the super-sized sandwich, a brightly painted jewelry box and festive, fabric wrapped vases.

30

Helpful Hints

* Spray the entire area with bug repellent prior to the party.
* To cut down on the chaos, set up several different entertainment areas.
* Consider asking friends to help organize and manage the events. If there is a pool or swimming hole, be sure to ask some friends to serve as lifeguards.
* Purchase a number of ribbons and/or inexpensive prizes to give to the winners of each event. (Be sure to include some consolation prizes for the wee ones.)

* Make or order the po-boy with a variety of fillings so there will be something for everyone. (Dooky Chase used ham, but you could use turkey, roast beef and "veggie".)
* If the food will be sitting out for a lengthy period, serve perishable condiments, such as mayonnaise, in individual packets - place them in an attractive basket or bowl.
* Music Suggestions: Camp songs and family favorites so everyone will want to sing along.

The flower-filled torchere.

A gigantic po-boy serves as both lunch and an unusual floral arrangement. An ebony urn holds napkins and cutlery.

Menu

Freshly Squeezed Lemonade
Soft Drinks, Beer and Minted Iced Tea

Sweet Potato Rolls
Stuffed Po-Boy or Submarine Sandwich*
Midori Melon Bowl *
Curry Chicken Salad *

Hand-cranked Ice Cream
Mini Desserts:
Old-Fashioned Bread Pudding with Bourbon Sauce
Fruit and Pecan Tarts

menu by Dooky Chase Restaurant

31

Fantasy Beach Dinner

Celebrate August with a fabulous, fantasy beach bash. A pink and white striped tent is the perfect place to savor the luminous, pastel-swirled sunset as it melts into the shining surf. Sip champagne and sample hors d'oeuvres served on the beach. Feel the early evening winds whispering off the water. Scrunch your toes into the silky sand that's still warm from the afternoon sun. Then heat up the night with an invigorating Latin or Caribbean beat. Serve dinner when you see the first twinkling of stars in the sky.

maracas, tambourines and brightly colored handkerchiefs and have the band lead the guests dancing in to dinner. Once the guests are seated, cool down the music to allow for comfortable conversation. Serve dinner. Before the dessert course, have the band play a song like "Old Time Rock and Roll" to get the guests on their feet and dancing. For the finale serve pineapple and banana flambé with vanilla ice cream. After coffee, cognac, and cigars, send guests home with their maracas as a lively reminder of an enchanting evening.

Here's how it works

Invite about 40 guests to come for cocktails shortly before the sun goes down. Set up a festive, striped tent on the sand as a sheltered spot for the appetizers and drinks. Sultry Latin music or a lively Caribbean beat from a steel band gets guests in the mood for the festivities to come. Encourage everyone to kick off their shoes and enjoy their libations on the beach barefooted. When the sun has set, change the tempo to "50's beach music". Pass out

Invitation

Hand-deliver hot pink mailing tubes tied up with a profusion of curling ribbon. Place pink and white striped peppermints inside the tube along with a scroll detailing the party particulars.

Place cards

Striped tent-shaped boxes filled with tissue and tart, tropic-inspired treats such as lemon squares and Key Lime cookies.

Hand-deliver hot pink mailing tubes with a whimsical card. Place card and envelopes are handpainted with watercolors.

A watermelon service plate.

32

August

Pink and white striped pavilion on the beach beckons guests to sip champagne and watch the sun set.

Menu

Appetizers & Drinks on the Beach
Champagne
Antoine's Smiles
Piña Colada
Frozen Peach Daiquiri
Prosciutto with Papaya
Shrimp Ravigote with Avocado *
Artichokes Aioli *
Display of Smoked Favorites: Sausage,
Pork Tenderloin and Baby Back Ribs with Hot Honey Dip

At the Table
Chardonnay
Chilled Breadfruit Vichyssoise
Crayfish Timbale on a Bed of
Exotic Greens with Hearts of Palm *
Lobster Thermidor *

Pineapple and Banana Flambé with Vanilla Ice Cream
Café au Lait, Expresso, Cognac and Cigars

menu by Antoine's Restaurant

A ring of flowers at the base of a metal palm tree centerpiece.

Decorations

A bright, pink, peppermint-striped pavilion makes an inviting oasis in the sand - complete with palm-capped tent poles and a diminutive chandelier. Palm trees also make their appearance on petite vases† filled with flowers and on centerpieces† encircled with blooms. Hand-painted tablecloths and napkins featuring palms, stars and hearts in watercolor hues add more delightful touches of tropical whimsy.

Helpful Hints

* To keep the bugs at bay, spray prior to the party and light citronella torches or candles.
* Have guests kick off their shoes for cocktails on the beach. Collect the shoes in a basket. Guests can pick them up as they go in to dinner or after the evening is over.
* Have the band members dress Ricky Ricardo-style.
* If you choose not to hire a band, play a particularly vibrant tune over the sound system for you, or an honoree, to lead the guests dancing in to dinner.
* Jimmy Maxwell's Music Suggestions: It's Rainin', Break Away, Chapel of Love, Blueberry Hill, Sea Cruise, I Heard it Through the Grapevine, Shout!, In the Still of the Night, My Girl, Old Time Rock & Roll, Love Potion #9, Your Mama Don't Dance, The Wanderer, Run Around Sue, Johnny B. Good, I Feel Good, Joy to the World, Rockin' Robin, I'm Walkin', Dancing in the Streets

Orchids and lilies adorn banana tree sculptures.

Tent box place cards

35

Pin cushion protea roses and dried hydrangeas decorate the table. Napkins are tied to masks that double as place cards.

Hand-deliver a menu from your favorite restaurant. At Mike's on the Avenue, you can even order a hand-painted silk tie designed by Mike Fennelly.

Entertaining in a Restaurant

There's something so invigorating about September - a certain thrumming excitement in the air. Summer finally sizzles to a close. Friends and family return from vacations and summer houses. The cultural season starts to percolate. The city seems to suddenly surge back to life. Surely a celebration is in order, but you really don't want to cook. It's the ideal time to indulge friends with a snazzy supper at one of the hottest spots in town.

Here's how it works

The true joy of entertaining in a restaurant is that aside from taking care of the guest list and paying the tab, all you really have to do is show up and enjoy yourself. However, to give your event added punch and a more personal flair, bring along some divine decorations such as place cards, favors, a centerpiece and perhaps even dramatic chair back bouquets. (This is when you become the "bag lady".)

Invite four to six friends for an enchanting evening at your favorite restaurant. (Make sure everyone understands that the evening is your treat so that there won't be any wrangling over the check.) Upon your arrival, arrange for a friend or dining companion to divert the other guests at the bar for a few minutes - this allows you to work your magic. Bring all the necessary goodies in a sturdy canvas bag and if necessary enlist the help of the wait staff. (The trick being that you must complete your table's fantastical transformation in five minutes or less.)

Guests may order from the menu or you may want to design a sensational set menu ahead of time. Be sure to end the evening with a flashy, "show stopping" dessert.

Invitation

Invite guests by phone. Then a few days before the big event, hand-deliver a menu from the restaurant tied with a pretty ribbon and a card detailing date, time and dress - guests will be primed for the evening and prepared to pick the perfect menu selections when it's party time. If you choose a set menu, ask the restaurant if you may have a couple of menus. Cover the insides of the menus using heavy paper and rubber cement then hand write all the party specifics. You could also

September

At Mike's on the Avenue in New Orleans, your table is a show-stopper with a 5 minute transformation.

Individual vases with delphinium, roses and gerbera daisies add another touch of color.

What could be easier than having specialty balloons tied to guests chairs? Colorful boxes filled with home made truffles are perched on Annie glass plates.

simply send out a lovely handwritten card that coordinates with your chosen theme.

Decorations

You may choose any decor or theme you desire for your dinner - let your imagination lead you. Here are a few, workable ideas to help get your creativity flowing.

Flowers and Fallen Leaves

Chic beverage bottles crowned with flowers make an instant centerpiece. Then for a fabulous fall touch, bring along a bevy of autumn-hued leaves to scatter across the table. (We used glass leaves.)

Balloons and Boxes

For an easy and inexpensive way to add panache to the table, order specialty balloons in fun shapes such as butterflies, fish, stars or hearts. Have them delivered to the restaurant and tied at varying heights to the back of your guests' chairs. Brightly colored boxes brimming with homemade treats such as pralines, fudge or truffles make marvelous take-home favors that double as place cards. Single blooms or small arrangements in unique, petite glass containers (use an odd number) help give the table a fresh look.

A Napoleonic Night

For an affair with French flair, have masks of Napoleon and Josephine printed prior to the party. Tie each mask with a Provençal-style napkin and set at each place setting.

Helpful Hints

* Menu cards make a pre-arranged meal extra-special (ask ahead if the restaurant can provide them). For a flattering touch consider having a dish named for a guest of honor.

* Always be sure to inquire ahead as to what extras your favorite eatery may be able to provide. (For example, Vicky Bayley, owner of Mike's on the Avenue in New Orleans has a fabulous collection of unusual and artistic china and glass pieces that can be requested for special events.) Chef Mike Fennelly, also at Mike's on Post in San Francisco, can even paint one-of-a-kind neckties for guests at both locations.

* Make arrangements for the check so it doesn't arrive at the table and interrupt the fun - take care of it in advance or have the restaurant send the bill.

* Visit the restaurant prior to the evening to scout out the perfect table. This also allows you to view the restaurant's chairs to determine if it's possible or practical to use chair back bouquets.

* For no-spill transport of flowers to the restaurant, nestle the arrangements carefully in the canvas tote. (For the six-pack, add flowers after it is already inside the tote; for individual vases pack them carefully around the praline boxes; and for the wire arrangement and chair back bouquets, place the arrangement in first then gently layer the bouquets on top.)

* Music Suggestions: Most restaurants don't mind playing your favorite tapes or CDs as long as they are in keeping with the general atmosphere.

For a quick decorating scheme, open one of the bottles in a six-pack of bottled water. Add flowers and place real or glass leaves all over the table.

Make a gorgeous centerpiece by decorating a miniature wire table and chair with French tulips and cabbage roses. A wonderful wire basket lined with moss also makes a nice alternative or just bring a simple vase filled with flowers.

Chair back bouquets cap off the decor with a touch of unexpected glamour. (These also make sensational gifts for your guests to take home and tie to their front doors.)

Menu

Pouilly-Fuissé:
Crawfish Spring Rolls
Barbecued Oysters with Pancetta
Roasted Chicken and Corn Quesadillas with
Saffron Creme Fraiche

Fumé Blanc
Chipolte Caesar Salad *
Crab Cakes served with Ancho Chili Mayonaise
and Salsa Fresca *

Port Wine
Crème Brûlée *

menu by Mike's on the Avenue

39

Pumpkin Carving Party

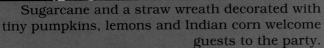

Sugarcane and a straw wreath decorated with tiny pumpkins, lemons and Indian corn welcome guests to the party.

Pumpkin containers are filled with maple and seeded eucalyptus leaves, sage, safflower, montbretia, cats paws and pumpkins on basil colored dowels

October is a month ripe for the senses. A rush of crisp autumn air. The sound of leaves rustling in the breeze. The distinct, almost heady, smell of lush harvest produce overflowing the open bins at the farmer's market. All these experiences mark the arrival of fall.

Instead of the annual family pilgrimage to pick the perfect pumpkin, celebrate the season by sharing the fun at a pumpkin carving gathering. Invite friends and their children to come in costume. There's a little pandemonium, but everyone goes home happy with their own freshly carved jack-o-lantern.

Here's how it works

Have this event up to a week before Halloween so that everyone can use the pumpkins created at the party in their decorations at home. Invite as many families as you feel you can comfortably accommodate - keeping in mind that pumpkin carving requires a good bit of space - and time. It's best to plan the party for early evening so there will still be enough daylight to hold the carving outside or on a porch.

It's nice to provide the pumpkins for your guests if possible, letting them pick their own from the dozens on display - or if not, simply request that everyone bring their own.

After everyone arrives, let the children pick their pumpkins and then start with the designing and carving as quickly as possible. Serve refreshments and let the children snack during the carving. The adults dine after the carving is complete. To keep the children entertained after the carving and while the adults eat, have a storyteller or encourage activities such as hide-and-go-seek, a costume parade or perhaps even a spontaneous play inspired by their attire.

When everyone is finished, line up all the pumpkins and light them for all to view. Be sure to buy plenty of votive candles to illuminate the carved creations and prizes (enough for everyone) to award for the prettiest pumpkin, the funniest, the scariest and so forth. (My sister, Marianne Mumford, always sends all the children home with live goldfish and fishfood.)

40

October

The fireplace is brimming with seasonal blooms. Antique quilts ablaze in autumn colors add a cozy, classic touch to the tables.

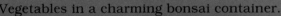
Vegetables in a charming bonsai container.

Invitation

Hand-deliver small pumpkins with the date, time and place inscribed in gold pen. Tie a note to the pumpkin stem with additional party information or include it in an envelope alongside. For another fun invitation idea, write the party information on miniature chalkboards including chalk and erasers. Then guests can use their slates to create pumpkin design ideas prior to the party. If you can find them, pumpkin carving sets make a festive addition to the invitation.

Decorations

Big bales of hay tied with wide, wonderful ribbon and piled with pumpkins and gourds make delightful decor - and provide extra seating. Place the hay and pumpkins at the front door and in various focal points throughout the house. Craft centerpieces by hollowing out pumpkins and/or large gourds and filling with flowers (see the How To section).

For festive place cards, use miniature bales of hay tied with ribbon (we got ours at a flower shop), petite pumpkins with the guests name

Table covered with an antique wedding ring quilt has a Brussels sprout topiary that can double as a place card.

42

emblazoned in gold ink or individual clay pots filled with fun Brussels sprout "bonsai".

Lagniappe
a little something extra...

Toasted pumpkin seeds make a splendid snack so save the seeds from the party.

<u>Toasted</u> <u>Pumpkin</u> <u>Seeds</u>
Ingredients:
fresh pumpkin seeds
1 tablespoon vegetable oil
salt

Clean fibers and pulp from the seeds. Wash seeds and pat dry. Pour the oil on clean hands and rub the seeds lightly with the oil. Spread seeds on a rimmed cookie sheet. Bake in a low oven about 200° F, shaking the pan occasionally, until seeds turn light brown (approximately one hour - but check the seeds from time to time because everyone's oven is different).

After removing the seeds from the oven sprinkle immediately with salt to taste (seasoned salt is also grand) shaking the pan to distribute evenly.

Helpful Hints

* Make sure you have several markers for designing, sharp knives for carving, large spoons for scooping and big bowls for holding the discarded pulp and seeds.
* Have lots of newspaper, butcher paper or drop cloths on hand as well to cover carving areas. Big garbage bags and loads of paper towels or dish cloths also come in handy.
* You might want to set up a special area for your clean-up station.
* Have the older children help supervise the younger ones.
* Serve dinner buffet-style.
* Realize that this party is pretty much "planned pandemonium" so just relax and enjoy it.
* Music Suggestions: The Muppets' Rainbow Connection, tapes of scary sounds, and then 50's songs or the Village People.

Menu

Sauvignon Blanc and Pinot Noir

Petite Acorn Squash Cakes topped with Brown Sugar and Aged Stilton Cheese, served warm, accented by Harvest Fresh Carved Gourds

Apple Cider Champagne Cocktail

Basil-Zucchini Muffins flavored with Parmesan Cheese * and Pumpkin-Pecan Muffins, both served with Honey Butter *

Raddichio, Watercress, Leaf Spinach and Arugula Salad Tossed with a Toasted Walnut and Sundried Cherry Vinaigrette

Oven Roasted Semi-Boneless Quail filled with Savory Chicken Stuffing, studded with Roasted Bell Peppers, French Shallots, Fresh Thyme and Crispy Bacon *

Sweet Onion Tart *

Pumpkin Caramel Custard with Candied Pumpkin and Praline Creme Anglaise *

menu by Joel's Grand Cuisine

Olivia Woollam and Ainsley Mumford create jack-o-lantern designs before getting a helping hand from their fathers with the carving.

November

Nothing could be finer than a feast in the fall...
The warm welcome of a table in the country.

Wild Game Dinner in the Country

It is Autumn at its finest. Fallen leaves blanket the ground with the gorgeous burnished tones of amber, magenta and ochre - and the cedar trees are a glorious golden brown. Smoldering embers of a fire crackle and glow. Tendrils of smoke waft lazily skyward and fill the chilled country air. The rich scent of roasting game fills the house. Hunting season is in full swing and suddenly the freezer is filled to the brim with game. It's the perfect excuse for a party, and the best part is that the men do the cooking!

Here's how it works

Invite 20 friends for an informal wild game supper in the country. Set up several tables - scattered imaginatively about - under the trees, in the garden, on the porch and in front of the hearth. Serve hot spiced cider, cold beer and hearty red wine. Encourage guests to stroll outdoors, play horseshoes and enjoy a relaxing afternoon. Have the men cook up the game. Ring the dinner bell at twilight.

An "inviting" scroll encrusted with ruby sealing wax and entwined with ivy is delivered along with a bottle of fine red wine.

45

Invitation

Deliver a split of good red wine encircled with ivy and accompanied by a stylish scroll, detailing the party particulars, and a map to the country location.

Decorations

This is the time to search your house. Peruse your walls, bookcases, closets, garden and garage gathering duck decoys, fishing lures, bird's nests, garden sculptures and any other intriguing items. Scatter these treasures throughout the decor to help create a casual "country chic" feel. Fall foliage, including cattails, nandina berries, ivy, heather and wild grapevine, is clustered in raised arrangements. Pots of yellow sage and other autumnal blooms also add color and warmth. Each table boasts its own identity - bare wood is ideal for an antique pine table, a regal tapestry tops another and a cheery Provençal-style print is perfect for a table set up outdoors. Hollowed apples crowned with indigenous wildflowers and leaves inscribed with gold pen serve as creative place cards. (You can also write directly on the apple.) Wine glasses are tied with heather and fall-toned ribbon or raffia

An apple ablaze with autumn blooms makes a festive place card.

Candlesticks clustered with plump, purple grapes, cattails tied to the napkins and some Old Paris oyster plates.

A flamboyant fall arrangement of heather, nandina berries, Gerbera daisies, cattails, wild grapevine, wild Italian ruskus, and wild yellow berries adds a divine, dramatic touch.

46

Antique fishing lures with a burnished leaf place card.

Helpful Hints

* Make sure game is cleaned and sausage prepared, and make the gumbo the day before. (Marinate venison overnight.)
* If you want to cook outdoors, use the grill and incorporate the oven as well when serving large groups.
* It's easier to decorate with ivy if it's conditioned first. Slice the stems and immerse entirely in water (the stems must also stay underwater). Soak the ivy overnight. To make sure the ivy is dry but remains fresh, remove from the water at least three hours before decorating, but leave the stems in water.
* To keep cattails from exploding and shedding, coat them lightly with hair spray. It is best to do this outside, on paper, away from the wind.
* Heather is marvelous for making long-lasting arrangements. Use it for decorating mantels, over doorways and for wreaths and front door displays. It makes a bit of a mess, but lasts well without water. We used it here and tucked it directly into ivy plants.
* To be in the best spirits - order your invitation splits and wine for the party by the case - often there is a case discount.

Some guests dine in the splendor of the Autumn foliage.

* Music Suggestions: Frank Sinatra, Louis Armstrong, Harry Connick, Jr. and Bobby Short (whose tape can be ordered from the Carlisle Hotel in New York City).

Menu

White Burgundy
Golden Roasted Oysters with Artichokes, Garlic and Parmesan Cheese*

Speckled Belly Goose Gumbo & Alligator Sausage over Rice and Chiffonade of Green Onions *

Pinot Noir or Zinfandel
Roast Rack of Venison *
Wild Mushroom and Four Bean Salad*

Champagne or Sauterne
Fig Tart *

menu by Commander's Palace

Black Tie Dinner Dance An Early Holiday Gift to Friends

Photo in picture frame serves as a place card and take-home favor.

Creating the invitation, votives and place cards with antique gold leaves, ribbon and copper wire.

Usher in the season in style by hosting an elegant, opulent evening of dining and dancing before your traditional decorations are up. It's a glorious gift to lavish upon your favorite friends during those calm, magical first days of the month.

Glamorous, gilded decor subtly hints at the holidays. Splendid champagne, sprightly piano music and a sumptuous repast are sure to get everyone in the spirit for the exhilarating rush of upcoming events. It's a grand, gala affair alive with merriment and energy.

Here's how it works

This party works best during the first days of December before the blitz of holiday activities. Invite friends for a black tie bash with all the trimmings - and tell them to wear their dancing shoes.

As guests arrive, each individual's photograph is taken and used later as a fabulous, framed place card that doubles as a take home party favor. Everyone mingles, enjoying the music, indulging in appetizers and sipping champagne. The ladies are each presented with a dance card to be filled with potential

Magnolia leaf charger, and handpainted star napkins with boxes as place cards.

Table in the living room laden with gold topiary and white camellias. Chairback bouquets adorn each chair.

partners prior to the ringing of the dinner bell. A fortune teller or Tarot card reader makes a festive addition to predict, for each guest, what the future and the new year will bring.

Supper is served, followed by a memorable finale of flaming café brûlot.

To add to the fun during the dining, after each course the hostess clicks her glass and invites the gentlemen to pick up their napkins and glasses and move to the next table. (This requires that each of your tables seats the same number of guests.)

After dinner it's time to "trip the light fantastic." Consider having a couple from a dance studio show off some different dance steps. Try the tango, the fox trot, the cha cha, the waltz and perhaps even some disco moves. Then encourage everyone to join in and dance the night away.

Invitations

Hand-deliver gilded, star-studded boxes of homemade fudge. Put the party particulars on a card tucked inside. Tie with glorious, golden ribbon. This is your early present to your guests! (These beautiful boxes also make marvelous place cards or take home favors.)

Decorations

This event is especially elegant dashed with winter white and glints of gold. Triumphant Casablanca lilies make a showy, yet classic, statement in "Celebration" chair back bouquets[†] and in towering "Celebration" table arrangements[†]. Flashes of gold appear everywhere from the star-spangled napkins and champagne flutes to the magnolia leaf chargers and topiaries.

Helpful Hints

* If you have a piano, engage someone to play music of different tempos throughout the evening. If you don't have your own piano, consider hiring a musician with a keyboard.

* If possible, enlist someone to help make the photo-place cards - perhaps an older child. Be sure to take each individual's photo, no couple shots.

* If there is no one to assist in the photo-place card crafting process you can always insert a white piece of paper into the frame with the guest's name written in gold pen (but photos make it all the more fun).

* You will need to clear an area large enough to accommodate dancing. This will certainly involve moving furniture. But be sure to leave a few chairs here and there for those that may want to sit out a song or two.

* Jimmy Maxwell's Music Suggestions: It Had to be You, Our Love is Here to Stay, The Lady is a Tramp, This Can't be Love, New York New York, Think of Me, What I Did for Love, I Love Paris, I Could Have Danced All Night, The Best of Times, I Just Called to Say I Love You, Just in Time, Love, You do Something to Me, As Time Goes By, Don't Get Around Much Anymore, Everything's Coming up Roses, What Kind of Fool am I?, Almost Like Being in Love, I've got the World on a String.

Glamorous, gilded decor subtly hints at the holidays.

Menu

Champagne
Salmon Tartare Canapés *
Miniature Oyster Newburg Bouchées

White Burgundy
La Chair de Crabes au Gratin *

Red Bordeaux
Le Coeur de Filet de Boeuf au Poivre *
Les Pommes de Terre Cocotte
Les Champignons Persilles
La Salade de Saison

Port
Les Fromages Assortis

Le Soufflé Glace Grand Marnier
Flaming Café Brûlot

menu by Arnaud's Restaurant

Entertaining Tips

* The guests are the most important ingredient in any party you give!
* Always use "the best" you can afford in food and beverage, etc.
* Do what you do best and leave the rest to professionals.
* End the party while people are still having fun - don't let it go on too long.
* Always have a favor or place card for guests to take home.
* Hand-deliver invitations or send a "show-stopper" invitation. It sets the tone for the party and lets people know that you have put forth some thought and effort.
* Music is a must! Begin the party with music at medium volume, turn it down for dinner, then up again for dancing. Make sure music is not so loud that it prevents conversation.
* Lighting is important. For an evening event, line the entranceway with torcheres, luminarias or up-lights. Dim the lights for dinner and light every candle in the house. Try not to have any light source at eye level. The answer is to use low votive candles or add shades to the candles to diffuse the light. For a dramatic effect accent trees, shrubs or even large house plants with tiny white lights.
* Flowers create excitement. Look around your house for your favorite items and "objets d'art" to incorporate into your theme or floral arrangement. Always take the setting of a flower arrangement into account. (Will it be in the center of the table, will guests be able to see each other over it, will it clash with a nearby work of art, etc.) Choose appropriate color, texture and height. Use unexpected and intriguing containers. Plant your garden so you can pick greenery and flowers all year.
* Hold your party in an unusual place. Examples include: airplane hanger, wine cellar, bowling alley, "dive" bar, railroad station, museum, zoo, railroad car, bank lobby, library, riverboat, ferry, yacht, museum, warehouse, streetcar or a trolley car...

Music

For live music, support your local musicians - seek out symphony performers, music school students and street musicians. Consider...

Jazz
Piano Players
Country and Western
Big Band
Harpists
String Quartets
Barbershop Quartets
Costumed Groups like the Andrews Sisters, The Four Tops, Diana Ross and the Supremes, etc.
Bagpipes
50's Bands
70's Bands
Frank Sinatra/Harry Connick Jr.
Juke Box
Disc Jockeys

Alternate Theme Ideas

Black and White Ball
Rouge et Noire Soiree
A Night in the Jungle
African Safari
A Night in Paris, London, Japan, Italy, Mexico, etc.
A Night on the Orient Express
Mardi Gras Theme
Top Hats and Canes
A Night on Broadway
Around the World in One Enchanted Evening
Cajun Party
Christmas in July

Boat Parade
Bahama Mamas
A Winter Wonderland
Roaring Twenties Speakeasy
Hollywood Greats
Medieval Feast
Clam Bake
Great Gatsby
Movie Themes - My Fair Lady, Dr. Zhivago, Star Wars
Tableaux Vivant
Come as Your Favorite Artist
Old South/Gone with the Wind

Jimmy Maxwell's Celebration Songlist

A Day in the Life of a Fool
A Train
After the Lovin'
Ain't Misbehavin'
Ain't That a Shame
Ain't She Sweet
Alexander's Ragtime Band
All My Rowdy Friends
All of Me
All the Things You Are
Almost Like Being In Love
Always
Always On My Mind
Angry
Anything Goes
Arthur's Theme
As Time Goes By
At Last
At the Hop
Avalon
Baby Face
Baby I Love You (Aretha)
Back in the U.S.A.
Ballin' the Jack
Basin Street
Because of You
Beal Street
Begin the Beguine
Behind Closed Doors
Best Is Yet To Come
Best of Times
Bewitched Bothered Bewildered
Beyond the Sea
Bill Baily
Birth of the Blues
Black Bird
Blue Bayou
Blue Eyes Cryin' in the Rain
Blue Moon
Blue Skies
Blueberry Hill
Body & Soul
Boogie Woogie Bugle Boy
Bourbon Street Parade
Boy From N.Y.C.
Brazil
Break Away
Breakin' Up Is Hard To Do
Brown Eyes Blue
Build Me Up Buttercup
But Not For Me
Butter & Egg Man
Button Up Your Over Coat
Bye Bye Baby

Bye Bye Blackbird
Cabaret
Cake Walkin' Babies
Called To Say I Love You
Can't Get Started
Can't Smile Without You
Candy
Can't Hurry Love
Caribbean Queen
Celebration
Chain of Fools
Chances Are
Changing Partners
Chapel of Love
Chattanooga Choo Choo
Cheek to Cheek
Chicago
China Town
Clarinet Marmalade
Conga
Could I Have This Dance
Crazy
Crazy Rhythm
Dada Strain
Dancin' in the Streets
Dancin' in the Dark
Dancing on the Ceiling
Daniel
Danny Boy
Dark Town Strutter's Ball
Day Tripper
Deep Purple
Desperado
Do You Know What It Means To
    Miss New Orleans
Dock of the Bay
Don't Get Around Much Anymore
Don't Sit Under the Apple Tree
Dr. Jazz
Dream
Dream a Little Dream of Me
Earth Angel
Edelweiss
Eight Nine Ten
Evergreen
Everybody Loves Somebody
Everyday I Get the Blues
Everything's Coming Up Roses
Fame
Fidgety Feet
Fire & Rain
Five Foot Two
Flash Dance
Foggy Day

For the Good Times
Forty Second Street
Freeway of Love
Frenesi
Friends In Low Places
From This Moment On
Georgia
Get Happy
Girl From Ipanema
Good Morning Heartache
Goody Goody
Green Eyes
Have You Ever Seen the Rain
Heard it Thru the Grapevine
Heartbreak Hotel
Heart of Rock & Roll
Heatwave
Heaven
Hello Dolly
Help Me Make it Through the Nite
Here's That Rainy Day
Hey There
High Heel Sneakers
Honey Suckle Rose
Honkey Tonk Women
How About You
How Deep is the Ocean
How Long Has This Been Goin' On
How Sweet It Is
Hully Gully
I Can't Begin To Tell You
I Can't Get Started
I Can't Give You Anything But
    Love
I Could Have Danced All Night
I Could Write a Book
I Don't Know Much
I Don't Wanta Walk Without You
I Feel Good
I Get a Kick Out of You
I Had the Craziest Dream
I Just Called To Say I Love You
I Know
I Left My Heart In San Francisco
I Love Paris
I Only Have Eyes For You
I Wanna Hold Your Hand
I Won't Dance
I'll Never Smile Again
I'll Remember April
I'm a Fool to Care
I'm Beginning to See the Light
I'm in the Mood For Love
I'm So Excited

I'm Walkin'
I've Got a Crush on You
I've Got a Lot of Living to Do
I've Got It Bad, That Ain't Good
I've Got Rhythm
I've Got You Under My Skin
I've Heard That Song Before
If I Had You
Iko Iko
In the Mood
Indian Summer
Is it True What They Say About
    Dixie
Isn't it Romantic
It Could Happen to You
It Had to be You
It's a Sin to Tell a Lie
It's All Right With Me
It's Been a Long Long Time
It's D'Lovely
It's Not Unusual
It's Only a Paper Moon
It's Rainin'
It's So Easy to Fall in Love
It's Too Late
Jambalaya
Jeeper's Creepers
Johnny B. Good
Joy to the World
Jump
Just a Gigolo
Just in Time
Just My Imagination
Just One Look (Ronstadt)
Just One of Those Things
Just the Two of Us
Just the Way You Are
Just You & I
Kansas City
Killing Me Softly
Knock on Wood
La Bamba
Lady in Red
Lady is a Tramp
Lady Marmalade
Laura
Lazy River
Leroy Brown
Let Me Call You Sweetheart
Lie Vie en Rose
Liebestrum
Like a Lover
Li'l Liza Jane
Listen to the Music

Jimmy Maxwell and his Orchestra...

A rare blend of musical talent, savior faire, and sheer magic. When society steps out, from the Sunbelt to the Big Apple, Jimmy Maxwell accompanies them. He's charmed Britain's Royal Family and delighted debutantes from San Francisco to Savannah. He plays it all: dance music from Broadway hits, swing sounds from the Big Band Era, nostalgia pieces from the 50's and 60's as well as New Orleans Jazz. Here are some of Jimmy Maxwell's favorites to give you a starting point in creating your songlist for your next celebration! Add your favorites to his...

Little Brown Jug	One Note Samba	Skylark	This Can't Be Love
Locomotion	One O'clock Jump	Slow Hand	Thousand Miles Away
Louie Louie	One, Two, Three	Small Hotel	Tie a Yellow Ribbon
Love	Oohh Baby Baby	So What's New	Tiger Rag
Love is Here to Stay	Orange Colored Sky	Somebody Loves Me	Till There Was You
Love Will Keep Us Together	Our Love is Here to Stay	Some Changes Made	Time of My Life
Lullaby of Broadway	Out of Nowhere	Someday Sorry	To All the Girls I Loved Before
Mack the Knife	Over the Rainbow	Someone to Watch Over Me	Tonight I Celebrate My Love
Makin' Whoopee	Paper Doll	Sometimes I'm Happy	Took Advantage of Me
Mama Don't Allow	Paper Moon	Somewhere Out There	Toot Toot Tootsie
Manhattan	Peg of my Heart	Somewhere Over the Rainbow	Tracks of My Tears
Mardi Gras Mambo	Pennies From Heaven	Song Sung Blue	Tulsa Time
Margaritaville	Pennsylvania, 6-5000	South Rampart Street Parade	Tutti Frutti
Margie	People Will Say We're In Love	Splish Splash	Tuxedo Junction
Marie Laveau	Pink Cadillac	St. James Infirmary	Twelfth St. Rag
Masquerade	Play That Funky Music White Boy	St. Louis Blues	Twilight Time
Meditation	Postman	Stairway to the Stars	Twist & Shout
Melancholy Baby	Pretty Woman	Stand By Me	Unchained Melody
Memory	Proud Mary	Stand By Your Man	Undecided
Midnight Hour	Put on a Happy Face	Stardust	Under the Boardwalk
Midnight in Moscow	Puttin' on the Ritz	Stars Fell on Alabama	Unforgettable
Millenburg Joy	Rain Drops Fallin' on my Head	Still of the Night	Walking to New Orleans
Midnite Special	Respect (Aretha)	Stompin' at the Savoy	Waltz Across Texas
Misty	Rhythm is Gonna Get Ya	Stormy Weather	Watch What Happens
Mona Lisa	Rock and Roll Music	Strangers in the Night	Way Down Yonder in New Orleans
Moonlight in Vermont	Rock Around the Clock	Street Where You Live	Way We Were
Moon River	Rockaby Your Baby	String of Pearls	Way You Do the Things You Do
Moonglow	Rockin' Pneumonia & the	Sugar Blues	Way You Look Tonight
Moonlite Serenade	Boogie Woogie Flu	Sugar Pie	What a Difference a Day Makes
More	Rockin' Robin'	Sugarpie Honey Bun	What a Wonderful World
Mother in Law	Rocky Top	Sukiyaki	What Did I Have
Mountain Greenery	Roll With It	Summer Samba	What I Did For Love
Muskrat Ramble	Route 66	Summertime	What'll I Do
My Blue heaven	Rum & Coca Cola	Summerwind	What's New
My Favorite Things	Run-a-Round Sue	Sunny Side of the Street	When I Die I'll Go To Texas
My Girl	S'Wonderful	Sunshine of My Life	When I Fall In Love
My Guy	San Francisco	Sweet Gypsy Rose	When Will I Be Loved (Ronstadt)
Natural Woman	Satisfaction	Sweet Lorriane	When You're Smiling
Near You	Saving All My Love For You	Taking A Chance on Love	Where or When
Never on Sunday	Scotch & Soda	Tangerine	Why Do Fools Fall in Love
New York New York	Secret Love	Teach Me Tonight	Will You Still Love Me Tomorrow
Nice Work (If you Can Get it)	Sentimental Journey	Tennessee Waltz	Wind Beneath My Wings
Night & Day	Serenade in Blue	Thank Heaven for Little Girls	Whiskey River
Nobody Till Somebody Loves You	Shadow of Your Smile	That Old Black Magic	Witchcraft
Nobody's Sweetheart Now	Shake Rattle & Roll	That'll be the Day	Woolly Bully
Old Black Magic	She Works Hard for the Money	That's a Plenty	Yesterday
Old Cape Cod	Sheik of Araby	The Christmas Song	Yes Sir That's My Baby
Old Man River	Shine	The Days of Wine & Roses	You Always Hurt the One
Old Rockin' Chair	Shout	The Look of Love	You Love
Old Time Rock & Roll	Silhouette on the Shade	The Rose	You Do Something To Me
On a Clear Day	Since I Fell For You	The Shadow of Your Smile	You Made Me Love You
On the Road Again	Since You've Been Gone (Aretha)	The Very Thought of You	You Send Me
On the Street Where You Live	Singin' in the Rain	The Wanderer	You Stepped Out of a Dream
Once in a While	Sittin' in the Ya Ya	This Boy	You Took Advantage of Me

January

Tulle Tablecloth

Purchase a piece of red tulle large enough to cover the table (allowing for a 12-inch drop on all sides) and several dozen silk flowers (red geraniums look especially divine). Cover table with butcher paper (allowing a 12-inch drop on all sides). Then cover the butcher paper with wax paper and then top with the tulle. Use masking tape to mark each place setting on the tulle to avoid gluing flowers where the plates will go. Hot glue flowers all over the tulle. After the glue dries remove the wax paper and butcher paper underneath and save for future projects.

Tulle Chair Covers

Follow the general directions for the tablecloth using any color tulle and any variety silk flower you desire.

Tulle Napkin Petticoats or Place cards

Cut a square piece of tulle or netting approximately 2-inches larger than the napkin. Hot glue silk flowers to one corner of the tulle. Put the napkin down on top of the tulle "petticoat" and fold corner to corner. To use the petticoats as place cards, tie on a name card with a pretty ribbon.

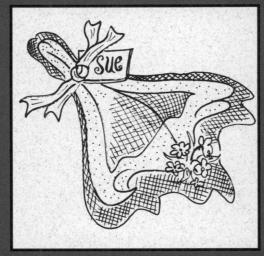

Centerpiece

Hot glue moss to the sides of a solid-sided plastic plant flat (21½" x 11"). You can get plastic plant flats at any nursery.

Add a couple of blooming plants (use 4-inch pots) to the container, then fill in with a colorful assortment of vegetables. Heap more vegetables outside of the moss container. Consider adding some blooms in individual water vials amongst the vegetables.

For extra flourish you may want to cap off the centerpiece by tying the container with a festive ribbon and finishing with an oversized bow.

Handpainted Aprons

Purchase white butcher aprons† at your favorite restaurant supply store. Decide on a design or theme or make each apron an individual work of art. (If you're feeling crunched for time you may want to simply personalize each apron with each guest's name.) Use paint specifically fashioned for fabric use. (We used Plaid Fashion Fabric Paint - it has a built-in tip for writing or you can simply squeeze some out and use a brush, depending on the look you want to achieve. The directions say to prewash the project, but we didn't and the paint still held up. We did, however, wait well over a week after the party before washing the aprons.)

February

Card-Making Table

Fill your table with everything you might need to create the perfect Valentine's card: card stock (red, fuschia, purple, pink and white), paper doilies, lace, vintage Valentines, colored markers, watercolors, heart garland, Valentine stickers of cherubs and hearts, etc., gold and silver pens, old magazines, glue, scissors and so forth.

Flower-Arranging Table

This table should have everything you might need to craft a sensational flower arrangement: flowers and greenery, floral wire, floral clay, oasis, marbles and clippers.

Food Preparation Area

(This area requires a good bit of space.)

You will need: heart-shaped cookie cutters in a variety of sizes, four cutting boards, cellophane wrap (preferably pink), several very sharp knives, two trimmed beef tenderloins, two loaves of unsliced bread, fresh, uncooked asparagus (enough for two small bundles per guest), two bunches of green onions, three-four red peppers, two (9x15) pans of Mississippi Mud, melted butter, six pouches of heart-shaped pasta wrapped in red tulle and tied with ribbon and six small jars of pesto (make your own or use store-bought).

Beef Cutting Board

Pre-slice the tenderloins into 1½ inch pieces. Trim off any excess fat. Each person cuts their two filets into heart shapes and wraps them in cellophane.

Vegetable Cutting Board

Prepare red peppers ahead of time. Stand each pepper upright, slice off the four sides of the pepper, discard the core. Each person will use the smallest cookie cutters to punch out several heart shaped pieces of pepper to use as garnish. For the asparagus bundles cut thin, flat strips of green onion or leek and carefully tie around the desired number of asparagus. Wrap all the vegetable goodies in cellophane.

Don't forget to add the pasta that's been wrappped in red tulle and the small jars of pesto.

Bread Cutting Board

Pre-cut your loaves into 1½ -inch wide slices. Each guest creates heart-shaped pieces using the cookie cutters. The shaped bread is then dipped into the melted butter and toasted in the oven at 250° F for about one hour. When the heart-shaped toasts are cool, wrap them in cellophane.

Dessert Cutting Board

Each guest creates two heart-shaped pieces of marbleized Mississippi Mud from two square pieces using knives or cookie cutters. Wrap in cellophane. (The Mud has been made the day before, with fudge sauce drizzled on top and allowed to cool, left uncut in the pan.)

Tulle Chair Covers

Drape approximately three yards of tulle over each chair. Slip wax paper between the chair and the tulle. Hot glue silk flowers all over the back and sides of the tulle chair cover (or glue all the flowers in one area at the top of the chair back to fashion a bouquet). Remove the wax paper and tie the cover to the chair with ribbon. (You will need about nine feet of ribbon to create a truly spectacular bow.)

Galax-Covered Chargers

This is a complicated craft, so consider it optional unless you have the time. (Directions are for one charger.) Buy heart-shaped oasis† . (If you cannot find heart-shaped oasis fill a heart-shaped cake pan with oasis.) Soak the oasis in water overnight. You'll need about 7 or 8 packs of galax leaves or approximately 40-50 leaves per charger. (Galax leaves can be purchased at floral supply and craft stores.) Divide leaves into small, medium and large. Cut the stems to approximately ½-inch in length. Then starting with the larger leaves, work from the outside edge in, covering the heart-shaped oasis with the leaves (see illustration). Attach the leaves by poking the stems into the oasis. Work all the way around the perimeter of the heart and then start the next row, gradually decreasing the size

of the leaves. Overlap the leaves slightly, making sure all the leaves go in the same direction and work around and around the edge, finishing in the center. Use smaller, shorter leaves on the part of the heart that goes in and use a pointy leaf to make the point of the heart.

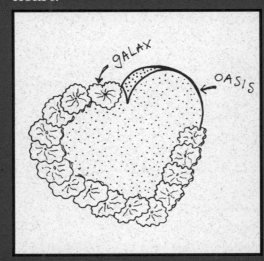

(You may use ivy leaves as a substitute; but since ivy stems are not as sturdy as the galax stems, the ivy leaves will have to be attached with floral pins.) You may want to add a small cluster of flowers to the charger for extra punch - but, be sure to leave enough room for the plate.

March

Boot Centerpiece

Pour approximately one cup of marbles into the toe of a favorite boot. Then fill a glass or similar container half full with water and insert into the leg of the boot, adding more marbles to help hold the glass in an upright position. Finally, arrange a fun assortment of curly willow branches, sunflowers, delphinium and godesia (or any other seasonal blooms that might strike your fancy) inside the container.

Skillet Centerpiece

Fill a black, cast iron skillet with water-soaked oasis. Then arrange red godesia and sunflowers in the oasis (low and tightly packed together.) Then, to give the arrangement some height, add either three to five irises. Add a bow to the skillet handle.

Hot Sauce Invitations/Place cards

Tie a sprig of statice and a small card detailing the party plans (or a place card) to each bottle of hot sauce using fun, bright ribbons.

Napkin rings

Purchase grapevine rings (approximately 2-inches in diameter) and silk flowers from a craft store. (For an alternate look, or if you cannot find the grapevine rings, detach the long leaves from silk tulip flowers, roll them lengthwise and hot glue together to make a fabric ring.) Hot glue a silk sunflower to each grapevine or fabric ring.

Canvas Leaves

(These can cover a tablecloth or be used as a place mats.) Cut three leaves - small, medium and large, from an elephant ear plant. Be sure to include at least a small portion of the stem with each leaf. Trace the three sizes of leaves repeatedly on a large piece of gesso-backed canvas (available at any art supply store) until the canvas is completely covered (about a dozen leaves). Cut the leaves out of the canvas. Spread leaves on drop cloth and paint one at a time with acrylic paint. (We used alternating jewel-tones of red, emerald, purple and fuschia.) Working fairly rapidly before paint dries, run your finger down the center of the wet leaf to make

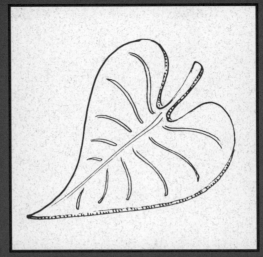

the center vein. Then using a paint brush (1 to 1½-inch thick with stiff bristles) make sweeping, outward strokes on each side the center stem. After the leaf is covered with the sweeping strokes use your finger to draw the smaller veins. When the canvas leaves are thoroughly dry, coat with satin-finish clear polyurethane. (After time and use the edges of the leaves tend to fray a little, simply trim and spray with polyurethane again.)

Paper Flowers

Go to your favorite party supply store and buy big brightly colored Mexican crepe paper flowers in every color of the rainbow. Arrange in galvanized containers that are filled with styrofoam.

Boxwood Container

Cover the sides of any small, square container with floral sticky tape - use one continuous strip of tape at the top of the container and one continuous strip at the bottom. Cut pieces of boxwood in lengths approximately one-inch higher than the height of the container.

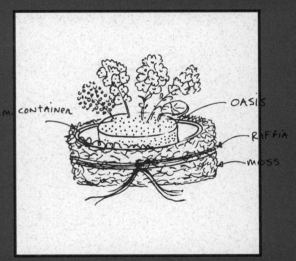

Peel the protective paper off of the tape and stick the boxwood to the container; continue until the entire container is covered with the greenery. Tie raffia around the boxwood covered container to secure. (You'll need about ten strips of raffia per container.) Tie each piece into a bow, leaving generous tails on the bows. Add oasis that has been soaked in water, then add flowers. (We used hydrangeas, snowball viburnum and galax.)

Chair Back Bouquets

Use aspidistra leaves as the base and then tie other flowers and greenery to the leaves with French, wired ribbon. (It is best to use flowers and greens that last well out of water including yarrow, magnolia leaves and bear grass.) Wire a bouquet to the back of each chair. Cover the exposed wire on the inside of each chair with a piece of ribbon tied into a neat knot or bow. Write each guest's name on an aspidistra leaf in each bouquet with a gold pen.

Aspidistra Leaf Stirrers

Use raffia to attach one pretty aspidistra leaf to each silver serving spoon. Lay the spoon down to see how the leaf falls and then write the name of each drink (Mimosa, Milk Punch, Gin Fizz, etc.) on the leaf in gold pen.

May

Cabbage Invitation

Find a big, leafy cabbage, slice off bottom. Insert small, plastic, water-vials of roses and delphinium between the leaves. Place in terracotta saucer with seed packets.

Gardening Apron

Buy sturdy, inexpensive aprons†. (Aprons can be purchased at many restaurant supply companies.) Tape stencil down tightly to the apron with masking tape, then cover the rest of the exposed fabric. Airbrush or spray paint the design onto the apron. Repeat until desired look is achieved. (You may want to hand-paint your design on the apron with fabric paint instead, if so see apron instructions in How To for January.) We used Design Master Basil #676 spray paint. When the apron is dry, add seed packets, gloves and any other gardening goodies to the pockets.

Gardening Gloves

Purchase cloth gardening gloves. Hot glue silk flowers to the wrist of each glove.

Trellis Centerpiece

Line the inside of a rectangular box (approximately 5-inches high x 7-inches wide x 18-inches long) with heavy plastic. Then carefully hot glue living or dried moss to the exterior of the box until the box is entirely covered. (Moss is available at many florists and floral supply stores.) Cut 2-inch thick styrofoam so that it fits snugly inside the box.

Secure a small piece of bamboo or gardening stake to each side of a 16" x 38" trellis using green floral tape. The bamboo or stakes should extend 2-3 inches beyond the end of the trellis in order to penetrate the styrofoam.

Spray paint the entire trellis. (We used Design Master Basil #676). When dry, place the trellis inside the moss-covered box.

Add small potted plants on one side of the trellis and water-soaked oasis on the other. (The plants and oasis should keep the trellis from wobbling. We used potted dahlias and added roses delphinium, ranunculus and tendrils of ivy to the oasis.) Twine ivy in and out of the trellis.

Silk Flower Pen and Pad Place card

Buy pens and notepads with a hole at an office supply or discount store. Buy large, pretty silk flowers such as Gerbera daisies, tulips or roses. Attach one big bloom to the top of each pen by taping the stem down the side of the pen with green floral tape. Neatly tape all the way down the pen until it is completely covered. Write each guest's name on the pad then stick the pen into the hole.

Chairs

Sand folding chairs lightly then spray with dark green paint. (We used Design Master Basil #676.) If desired, hot glue patches of moss all over the seat of the chair to cover (the drawback being that some of the moss will end up on your guests after they sit down, but

then we all have to suffer for creativity). Tie chairs with festive ribbon.

June

Pattern for palm trees. (These can be enlarged on a photocopier to various sizes.)

Sunflower Baskets

Purchase inexpensive wicker or basket-style plate holders and silk or paper sunflowers. Snip the stems from the fake flowers with scissors or, if necessary, with wire cutters. Then hot glue the flowers around the rim of the plate holders. (For another

attractive look simply glue a grouping of the flowers together on one side of the plate holder.) Place brightly-hued napkins inside the plate holder.

Beach Totes

Make a bouquet using whatever fresh greenery and flowers you can find in your yard or at your florist. (We used aspidistra, sunflowers, Gerbera daisies and palms.) Tie the bouquet with bright ribbon and attach to the tote with florist wire.

Pattern for fish. (Other patterns available at fine party and stationery stores.)

July

Cocktail/Snack Tables

Place a circle, cut out of ½-inch thick plywood (approximately 24 inches in diameter), on top of each wooden, (TV tray sized), folding tray. Cover each table with a double bed sheet and top with a square of contrasting fabric. (If you don't sew, pink the edges of the fabric with pinking shears.) Add flower arrangements in unusual containers on each table.

Torcheres

Purchase several inexpensive bamboo torcheres (ours came from Pier One). First, remove the oil can from the torchere. Cut and carefully remove the rings and pieces holding the oil can. Recycle the oil can. Then lightly sand the bamboo.

Take a piece of cardboard (we used the light cardboard that comes with new shirts) and cut it into 3-inch x 2-inch pieces. Cut notches into one of the 2-inch sides of the cardboard, then square off the top by cutting across all the notches (see diagram). This will be used to create the "striae" effect. Stick the torchere in the ground and paint with green water-based paint. Let dry. Cover the torchere with blue paint and, working quickly while the paint is still wet, drag the cardboard comb over the torchere to create a striated look. (We used Benjamin Moore latex paints in lime green and azure blue that we had mixed - if you bring a paint store this book or a sample of fabric that you like they can help you match it.) Continue combing, wiping off any excess paint off the comb as you go, until the entire torchere is streaked. Let dry completely, then spray with satin polyurethane. Place a small vase or jar in the spot previously occupied by the oil can. Add your favorite flowers. We used allium, roses, delphinium, button chrysanthemums, peonies and Boston fern.

Handpainted Jewelry Box

Purchase an inexpensive jewelry box (ours came from the Bombay Co.). Sand the box well and paint with a white stain resistant paint such as KILZ or BIN. When dry, lightly sand the box again with fine-grained sandpaper.

Paint the box with green latex paint first. Let dry completely. Apply the blue paint in sections. (We used the same blue and green water-based paints we used on the torcheres.) Drag a cardboard comb (see instructions for torcheres) evenly over the wet blue paint to create a striated effect. Then paint another section and repeat this step until the entire jewelry box is covered. Let dry. Spray with satin polyurethane and let dry. Add flowers (they must be in small containers filled with water). We used Lady's mantle, pink peonies, button chrysanthemums, hydrangea and lemons.

Fabric-Wrapped Vase

Buy an inexpensive vase at a discount store. (The color is unimportant, but the shape should be a traditional, slender, ginger-jar style.) Cut a square of fabric approximately 54-inches x 54-inches. Lay the square of fabric face side down. Place the vase in the center of the fabric. Fold the corners of the fabric in towards the center. Then pull each side of the fabric up, one by one, until you are holding them all. While still holding the fabric, slip a large rubber band over the fabric, around the neck of the vase. (It is helpful to have someone to assist you with this.) Gather the material evenly at the top. Then finish off by tying with glamorous ribbon or cording to cover the rubber band. (We added cording with tassels).

Flower Bedecked Po-Boy or Submarine Sandwich

Buy or make, if you dare, a six to eight foot poorboy or submarine-style sandwich. (We bought ours from Subway and it comes on a stiff board which makes it easier to transport and decorate. You can also order the bread from a specialty bakery.) The sandwich should be covered in plastic wrap. Leave the wrap intact until ready to serve. When ready to add the flowers, use a sharp, serrated knife to cut out a portion of the sandwich (through the wrap) approximately 3½-inches wide by 6-inches in length (the cut-out may be smaller or larger depending on the size of the flower container you are using and the width of the sandwich). The container should fit snugly inside the hole. (We used inexpensive, slender, liner containers

available at most florist supply stores; but you can use anything you have on hand that fits the sandwich, from small jars to small margarine tubs and so forth). Add oasis, that has been soaked overnight, to the container. Add flowers and then put the entire creation in the hole in the sandwich. (Do not add any water after the arrangement has been placed in the sandwich; spilled water will make the sandwich soggy.)

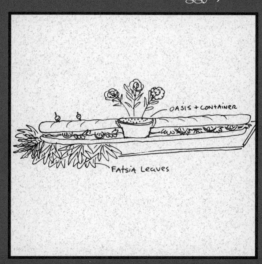

When you are ready to serve, unwrap the sandwich and tuck clean, fatsia leaves and other non-poisonous greenery underneath to decorate.

Handpainted Hydrangea Umbrella

(The one pictured in the month of July was painted by Judith Feagin) To paint your

own see instructions for painted cloth (the tablecloths and napkins) in "How To" for August.

August

Watermelon Service Plates

Slice watermelon into round slices about 1-2 inches thick (see illustration). Place each round on a plate (use plates that are as close to the size of the watermelon round as possible). Poke fresh flowers with sturdy stems into the watermelon rind. (We used anemones, delphinium and roses.) Serve the salad on the watermelon round and place other food in ramekins that fit on the top. (Ramekins can be found at Williams-Sonoma, Pier One Imports, etc.)

Tent Box Invitations/Place cards

Put together white cake boxes† (approximately 6-inches x 6-inches x 4-inches). Leave the box open with the side flaps and top flap erect. Fold side flaps and top flap in towards the middle slightly and tape the sides together with transparent tape. Draw tent patterns on the front, sides and back of the box with markers (see pattern). Cut a piece of fabric the size of the roof and glue it to the top of the box. Fill the box with brightly colored tissue paper and cookies or candy.

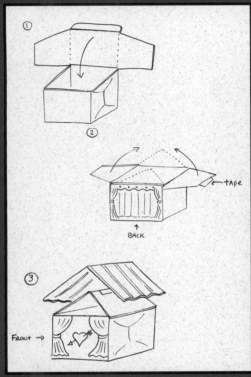

Add a card with the party information on it. (Or if the boxes are used at each place setting, add a place card or write each guest's name on a palm tree or flag taped to the front of the tent box.)

Handpainted Tablecloths and Napkins

Make or buy plain white tablecloths to fit 60-inch round tables (the cloth should be 120-inches in diameter to reach the floor.) Hem the cloths if necessary and wash to remove any sizing. Lay the fabric on a flat surface and draw your design on the fabric lightly with pencil. Retrace pencil lines with black laundry markers. Color in the designs with paint (We used Deka fabric paint and Design Master spray paints.) When the paint is thoroughly dry, put the cloths in the dryer (preferably commercial dryers) on high heat for at least an hour. Wash and paint napkins in the same fashion, coordinating the designs and colors with those on the tablecloths. (If you have any artist friends try to enlist them to help you with the designing and painting. It is best to dry clean the tablecloths after use.)

September

Handpainted Bag with Tulips and Leaves

You will need a colorful bag for transporting all your party supplies. If you have the time consider decorating a sturdy canvas bag with fabric paint to serve as your carryall (follow directions for the handpainted aprons in How To for January) or simply buy a snappy looking tote.

Flowers and Fallen Leaves Six-Pack Centerpiece

Buy a six-pack (or four-pack) of mineral water bottles, Leaving them in the carton, pour half of the liquid out of one of the corner bottles. Add flower arrangement to the open bottle. (We used viburnum, delphinium and geraniums.) You can certainly add flowers to any or all of the bottles but it makes it a bit more difficult to handle and transport.

Flowers and Fallen Leaves

Leaf Place cards

You can make quick place cards by writing guests names on leaves in gold pen (for the glass leaves we used black laundry marker.) You could attach each personalized leaf to a single bloom with ribbon or gold cording and use at the designated placesetting.)

Mask Place cards

Have masks duplicated at your local printer or copying store on heavy stock. Cut out the faces and staple each mask to a tongue depressor. Write each guest's name on the back of each mask and tie with a pretty napkin.

Chair Back Bouquets

Stunning chair back bouquets can be crafted by lining wire baskets with moss. Then add a sturdy, plastic water-proof liner. Place water-soaked oasis inside the basket (being careful that the oasis doesn't show). Add flowers (we used viburnum, cabbage roses, delphinium and parrot tulips) and finish your gorgeous creation off with an elegant ribbon.

October

Pumpkin Centerpieces

Cut the top off of each pumpkin and discard. Scoop out the pulp and seeds. Fill a glass or other suitable container approximately half-full with water, and place inside the pumpkin, surrounding it with bunched up paper so it stands firmly upright. Add flowers and greenery. (Safflowers, sage, montbretia, kangaroo paws, eucalyptus and maple leaves make marvelous seasonal selections.)

Brussels sprout Bonsai

Write guests names on small clay pots with gold paint pens. Fill each pot with styrofoam. Cover the top of the pot with a kale leaf. Put a green pick into the bottom of a Brussels sprout. Carefully peel the leaves of the sprout open. Stick the pick into the kale leaf covering the pot. Mist the "bonsai" sprouts so they remain fresh and attractive. (If possible, place in the refrigerator until an hour before the party.)

Vegetable Centerpiece in Bonsai Pot

Cut beautiful pieces of broccoli, broccaflower, Brussels sprouts, turnips and red onions to create a miniature vegetable forest.

Fill a bonsai container (or other attractive cache pot) with styrofoam. Cover the styrofoam with a thin layer of wet oasis and add purple kale leaves, and then the vegetables on 4" to 6" florist picks. Add more kale leaves for flourish if needed. Mist the arrangement and, if possible, put in the refrigerator until party time.

November

Raised Floral Arrangements

Purchase an inexpensive ivory or neutral toned vase and several metal bases. (There are many such bases available at floral supply, craft and discount stores or they can be ordered). Place potted plants of ivy in the metal bases and intersperse with heather. (The heather does not require water; it can be placed directly into the ivy.) Set the vase atop the tallest metal base and add arrangement. We used heather, nandina, Gerbera daisies, cattails, wild grapevine, wild Italian ruskus, and wild yellow berries. Pyracantha and curly willow also work well.

Apple Place cards

Core apples, adding a little lemon juice, to keep them from browning. (Slice the bottom off the apple if it tends to tip). Then place plastic, florist water vials that have been filled with water into each apple's center. Add flowers. (We used nandina berries, heather and indigenous wildflowers.)

Bird's Nests

These can be purchased at some floral supply and craft stores. Fill them with miniature eggs or speckled egg candy.

Grape and Ivy Entwined Candlesticks

Place candles in crystal candlestick holders. Entwine wire through the top of each grape cluster until securely fastened, leaving the two ends free to twist around the neck of the candlestick holder where it will meet the candle. Hide the wire by tucking pin-point ivy where necessary.

December

Star Studded Invitation Boxes

Put together 6x6x4-inch white cake boxes† - one for each couple invited. (You should be able to find them at most party supply stores.) Hand stamp the boxes with stars using gold ink, leaving room to add the guest's name later. (We used a star-shaped rubber stamp from Ballard Designs and Deka water-based enamel paint in gold.) You may need to touch-up the stars with a small paint brush. Personalize each box with the guests name. When the ink is dry, add gold, matte tissue paper, homemade fudge and the party particulars. Tie with gold ribbon and deliver.

Picture Frame Place cards

Trim Polaroid pictures, taken as guests arrive, and place in small, golden frames. Set each photo-place card at the designated placesetting.

Star-Studded Napkins

This project should be done a week or two in advance. Purchase the largest linen napkins you can find - preferably 20" or 22" square. Wash and iron napkins. Paint the border of the napkin, on both sides, with gold fabric paint (we used Deka). Then, using a rubber star-shaped stamp and the gold fabric paint, carefully stamp stars all over the napkin. (We used a star stamp from Ballard Designs.) You may need to touch-up the stars with a small paintbrush. Let dry completely, then put napkins in a clothes dryer (preferably a commercial dryer at a laundromat) on the highest setting for an hour. Iron napkins and put them on the table.

Gold Magnolia Leaf Chargers

Cut poster board into large circles (approximately 12½ inches in diameter). Spray the circles and magnolia leaves with gold paint. (We used Design Master Brilliant Gold #731.) Let dry. Then, working from the outside in, carefully hot glue the leaves in a circular pattern until you've covered the entire board.

Starry Champagne Flutes

(If possible practice your art skills on an old glass before beginning on the champagne flutes.) For best results wash flutes in the dishwasher using washing soda. (If you can't find washing soda, use your regular dishwashing detergent.) Let the flutes stay in the dishwasher until they are completely dry. Then using a cloth to hold the stem (your hands should touch the glass as little as possible), paint each flute. (We used Deka water-based enamel paint and the simple star design we all learn as a child.) When the painting is completed, invert the flutes on a cookie sheet and bake in the oven at 225 degrees for an hour. The finished flutes should always be hand-washed. (Another method of painting your glasses is Delta CeramDecor "Paint 'n Press" transfers, available at craft stores. Choose one of their designs and follow instructions.) For extra flourish, add gold ribbon tied into a bow at the base of each flute. (These glasses are great for using throughout the holiday season!)

Flower Pot Bases for Topiaries and Votives

(Wear plastic gloves.) Purchase 5-inch clay pots for the topiaries and several smaller clay pots to hold the votive candles (use tea lights that come in individual plastic containers). Place all the pots on a large drop cloth and spray with clear, fast-drying polyurethane spray (lightly on the interior and a good coat on the exterior). Let dry and spray a second time. Then take a clear, plastic, dress-length, dry cleaning bag and cut it into thirds. Bunch up one of the pieces of plastic and spray with gold paint, use this to lightly "pounce" the paint onto the pots. Then bunch up another piece and repeat the process with copper-colored paint. Bunch up the third piece and "pounce" on basil-colored paint. Then repeat the process again with a final "pouncing" in gold. (We used Design Master Spray Paints in Brilliant Gold #731, Copper #733 and Basil #676.) When the paint is dry lightly coat the pot with Antique Walnut Min-Wax. When the pots are dry add a final coat of clear polyurethane. (Note: The paint does not have to be totally dry before moving on the next "pouncing". The painting should be uneven and be sure to allow a touch of the terra-cotta color of the pot to show here and there. Use only a little bit of the copper and basil colors.)

Antique Gold Leaf Topiary Forms

Purchase topiary forms (cone-shaped and/or classic double and single ball forms) and antique gold Salal leaves† (You can find the forms and leaves at many floral supply or craft shops.) Spray paint the stem part of the topiary form. Divide the Salal leaves into small, medium and large. (Use the smaller leaves for the ball-shaped topiaries and for the top portion of the cone-shaped form.) Start at the top of the cone topiary.

Add two dots of hot glue to a small leaf, one at top and one at bottom, and place it at the top of the topiary form (use "low melt" glue sticks). Secure the leaf with a small straight pin. Then repeat the process placing another small leaf next to the first, allowing the edges to overlap.

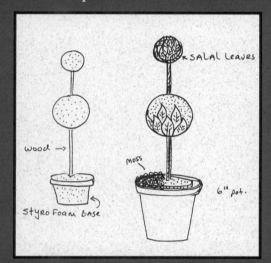

After completing the first row of leaves start the second row halfway down the first row. Hot glue, add leaf, secure with pin (if needed) and so forth, allowing each leaf to be overlapped by the next in the row. Gradually increase the size of the leaves you are working with. When you reach the last row of leaves wrap the base of the leaves underneath the bottom edge of the

styrofoam and tuck them all the way to the stem, so that the form is completely covered. Secure these leaves with straight pins.

Using only small leaves, cover the round ball form in the same fashion. Then add the forms to the dry painted pots. (You may need to trim a bit of the styrofoam in order to fit the forms snugly into the pots.) Add moss to the pot around the topiary form. Use as is or festoon further with ribbon and flowers.

Note: You can use lemon leaves but you will get a different effect. If using fresh, let the leaves dry naturally, and they will turn a beautiful moss green color. The leaves will be fragile and have a delightful, crinkly, ruffle-edged appearance. Fresh leaves must be attached to forms using tiny straight pins or spray glue, hot glue will burn the leaves.

ABCDEFGHIJKLM
NOPQRSTUVWXYZ

ABCDEFGHIJKLMN
OPQRSTUVWXYZ

These alphabet patterns are included so you can enlarge them on a photocopier if you want to trace them and transfer to your project using carbon paper. Or just copy them freehand for any projects you want to hand-letter.

Bacco Restaurant

Nestled in the French Quarter on Chartres Street, Ralph Brennan's Bacco Restaurant is a great Italian bistro with a New Orleans twist specializing in homemade pastas, wood-fired pizzas, and fresh regional seafood. Dine on Creole Italian gumbo, red bean ravioli, or seasonal Louisiana crawfish pizza while enjoying a stunning interior of gothic arches, Venetian chandeliers, handpainted murals and Baroque ceiling paintings. Breakfast, lunch, dinner and a festive Sunday jazz brunch are all served with a decidedly sophisticated and elegant flavor. The dress code at Bacco is New Orleans chic - from blue jeans to black tie.

Not only is Ralph Brennan a renowned New Orleans restaurateur, but he is also known for his community and business activism. He just received I.F.M.A.'s Gold Plate Award - the food service industry's highest operator's recognition.

Menu

Chardonnay
Mixed green salad with roasted pecans
Shrimp with Penne Pasta *
Roasted Chicken with Pesto Cream *

Red Zinfandel
Duck Raviolis with Shiitake Mushrooms *

Fume Blanc
Mussels and Linguine *

White Chocolate Lasagna

menu by Bacco Restaurant

return to pot. Pour shrimp mixture over pasta and toss well, adjust the seasoning and place in warm bowls. Garnish with freshly chopped Italian flat leaf parsley.

Roasted Chicken with Pesto Cream over Pasta

Ingredients:
1 - 3 lb. fryer chicken
1/2 cup pesto
1 quart heavy cream
1/4 cup Parmesan cheese (Parmigiano - Reggiano)
1/4 cup Romano (Pecorino) cheese
2 lbs. angel hair pasta
toasted pine nuts
kosher salt
freshly ground black pepper

Preparation:
1) Take the chicken and rinse off outside and inside the cavity. Pat dry. Season inside with salt and pepper, then put in a half of lemon and five cloves of garlic.
2) Truss chicken and roast at 375° F. for 40 minutes. When done (should register 160° F. on a meat thermometer) let cool, then pick meat (discarding the skin) into bite sized pieces.
3) In a large pot, place cream and put over medium heat. Reduce cream by quarter. While cream is reducing put on another large pot of salted boiling water to cook pasta in.
4) To your cream, add the pesto then add both cheeses and whisk until all the cheese is melted. Add in your picked chicken, and season with salt and pepper to taste.
5) When pasta is done, drain and return to the pot. Pour 3/4 of the pesto sauce over pasta and toss.

Shrimp with Penne Pasta

40 shrimp (31/35 per pound size), peeled and deveined
1 cup tomato sauce
1 medium yellow onion, diced
1 small green bell pepper, diced
1 clove garlic, chopped
2 Tbs. capers
3 Tbs. calamata olives, pitted and sliced
1 lemon, zested
2 Tbs. extra virgin olive oil
1/2 cup white wine
1 cup shrimp stock
2 lbs. penne pasta

1 tsp. kosher salt
1/2 tsp. freshly grated black pepper

Preparation:
1) Fill a large pot with water and place on high heat.
2) In a large sauté pan, place in olive oil and put on medium-high heat. Add onion, cook until soft, add bell pepper and garlic and cook for one minute.
3) When water boils, add 1 Tbs. salt and penne and cook until al dente.
4) Add the shrimp to the sauté pan and toss. Deglaze with white wine and add remaining ingredients.
5) When pasta is done, drain and

Place pasta in warm bowls and ladle remaining sauce over top.
6) Garnish with toasted pine nuts and a nice floret of fresh basil leaves.

Pesto

Ingredients:
2½ cup basil leaves, tightly packed then washed
4 Tbs. pine nuts
3 cloves of garlic, finely chopped
¾ cup parmesan cheese
3 Tbs. Romano cheese
¾ cup extra virgin olive oil

Preparation:
1) Place basil, olive oil, pine nuts, garlic, and a pinch of salt in a food processor.
2) Turn on and process until smooth.
3) Add cheeses and process until just incorporated.

Duck Raviolis

Ingredients:
1 lb. roasted duck, pulled apart
1 medium yellow onion, finely diced
1 clove garlic, finely chopped
1 Tbs. Parmesan cheese
2 Tbs. extra virgin olive oil
½ tsp. salt
¼ tsp. freshly ground black pepper
bread crumbs
fresh pasta sheets

Preparation:
1) In a bowl, place the duck meat and set aside.
2) Pour oil in a sauté pan and place on high heat. When hot, add onion and cook until softened. Add garlic,

cook for a minute and remove from heat. Let cool.
3) When cooled, add onion mixture to the duck along with cheese, salt, and pepper.
4) Add just enough bread crumbs to help bind mixture, and adjust seasoning.
5) Lay out a pasta sheet and brush lightly with an egg wash.
6) Place filling in dollops about an inch apart in a single row on the pasta sheet (approximately one ounce per portion).
7) Fold over pasta and press around filling, being sure to get out all the air. Cut out raviolis.
8) When raviolis are done, they can be cooked in salted boiling water for approximately 2 minutes.

Shiitake Mushroom Sauce

Ingredients:
1 lb. Shiitaki mushrooms, julienned
1 clove garlic, sliced thin
2 Tbs. extra virgin olive oil
¼ cup white wine
½ cup chicken stock
2 Tbs. unsalted butter
pinch crushed red pepper
¼ tsp. salt
1 Tbs. fresh sage, julienned
freshly ground pepper to taste

Preparation:
1) Place a sauté pan over medium high heat. Add the oil and when heated, add the garlic. Move the garlic around until it is golden brown over the whole surface.
2) Add mushrooms and sage and sauté for one minute.
3) Add white wine. When wine is almost evaporated, add chicken stock, crushed red pepper, salt, and black pepper.

4) Cook for another minute and add butter and adjust the seasoning.
5) Add duck raviolis to the sauce and serve.

Mussels and Linguine

Ingredients:
32 each mussels, washed and debearded
1 cup ripe tomatoes, diced
2 cloves garlic, chopped
1 cup white wine
4 Tbs. extra virgin olive oil
2 Tbs. fresh basil, chiffonaded
½ cup fennel bulb, julienned
1 shallot, finely chopped
1 tsp. kosher salt
¼ tsp. freshly ground black pepper
pinch crushed red pepper
2 lbs. linguine

Preparation:
1) In a large enough pan or pot to hold all of the mussels, place oil and put over high heat.
2) Place another pot filled with water on high heat to cook pasta.
3) When oil is hot, add fennel, tomatoes, shallots, and garlic and sauté for one minute.
4) Add mussels, white wine, and basil. Cover and let steam.
5) When the water comes to a boil, add 1 Tbs. salt and cook linguine until al dente and drain.
6) When mussels open, turn off heat and remove mussels.
7) Add pasta into sauce and toss well. Place pasta on warm serving plates and then mussels around pasta. Pour any remaining sauce over pasta and serve.

February

Bev Church

I learned to cook from my mother. She had a wonderful flair and created her own recipes, also serving a few from my grandmother. Our styles of entertaining are very different but I use her recipes all the time. She makes great gumbo, étouffée, Oysters Rockefeller, and sinful fudge and pralines. Mom would invite 30 to 50 friends for dinner by telephone and always served buffet style. The florist was called to do the flowers and she attended to all other details.

I love to have seated dinners for 8 to 12 with hand-delivered invitations, painted glasses and napkins as favors. I create the tablescapes complete with flowers and cook as many courses as I can. If I don't have the time, I cater, or go get "take-out," but I'll always cook one course! The fudge and praline recipes are added because I'm always talking about hand-delivering special packages of fudge or pralines...

Enjoy!

Dinner á Deux Menu

Champagne
Oysters Rockefeller *

Asparagus Bundles tied with Green Onion
Strips garnished with Red Pepper Hearts

Heart-Shaped Pasta with Pesto

Heart-Shaped Filet Mignon
with Crawfish Etouffée *

Marbleized Mississippi Mud with Hot
Fudge Sauce *

menu by Bev Church

Oysters Rockefeller

2, 10 oz. bags washed fresh spinach, stems removed
10 green onions, tops and bottoms
1 stick melted butter
1/2 cup olive oil
1 cup Worcestershire sauce
1 Tbs. Tabasco sauce
1/2 cup catsup
1 Tbs. Tony's Seasoning
1 1/4 cup tightly packed chopped parsley
1 1/2 cups chopped celery, tops only

2, 2 oz. tubes of anchovy paste
6 cloves garlic, chopped
1, 10 oz. can of bread crumbs
1 dozen oysters per person

Melt the butter and add olive oil. Add the other liquid ingredients and stir. Put some spinach, green onions, garlic, celery and parsley into a blender. Do not pack too tightly. Pour some of the liquid and start the blender. Keep adding all ingredients alternating liquid and greens and pour as you go into a large mixing bowl. When all is liquefied, add the bread crumbs and mix. Let sit over night to let the flavors go through. Drain oysters and place 1 dozen in each individual ramekins. Put the Rockefeller sauce on top. Bake at 400° F in the oven until bubbling. Serve immediately.

* You may also use this sauce on top of tomatoes. Slice the tops off and add 1/2 cup of sauce. Bake at 350° F for about 15 min. Makes about 20 tomatoes.

Crawfish Etouffée

This will serve 8, freezes well)

Ingredients:
3/4 stick of butter or 3/4 cups of olive oil
3/4 cup of flour
2 cloves of garlic, chopped
1 cup of celery, chopped
2 cups of onions, chopped
1 (28 oz.) can tomatoes, crushed
3-4 bay leaves
1/2 cup green onions with tops
1 tsp. thyme
1 Tbs. Tony's Seasoning (or to taste)
2 Tbs. Worcestershire sauce
2 lbs. crawfish tails
1 cup liquid (white wine or water)
1 Tbs. lemon juice
1/8 cup jalapeño slices (optional)
Tabasco sauce to taste

Preparation:
1) Make a walnut colored roux with butter and flour.
2) Add garlic, celery, onions, bay leaves, and thyme.
3) Sauté uncovered for 30 minutes over low heat.
4) Add tomatoes, pepper, salt Tabasco, Worcestershire sauce, jalapeño slices, and liquid and cook for 45 min., stirring occasionally.
5) Turn off fire and add crawfish tails and lemon juice.
6) Let chill overnight to allow flavor to marinate thoroughly.
7) When ready to serve, heat to boiling then serve over filet mignon or rice.
8) Garnish with green onion tops.

Marbleized Mississippi Mud with Fudge Sauce

2 sticks real butter
2 cups sugar
1 1/2 cups flour
1 tsp. baking powder (added to flour)
4 eggs
2 tsp. vanilla
12 oz. semi-sweet chocolate chips
1 cup chopped pecans
10 oz. miniature marshmallows

Melt butter and add sugar. Stir well. Add flour mixed with baking powder and eggs alternating each, and beat well after each addition. Add vanilla and stir. Pour into 9" by 13" greased pan and sprinkle with chocolate chips. Bake for 25 to 30 minutes at 350° F. Do not over bake. Remove from oven and sprinkle with marshmallows and nuts. Let melt together and top with following sauce.

Hot Fudge Sauce for Marbleized Mississippi Mud

1 box confectioner's sugar
1/3 cup half and half
2 squares bitter chocolate
1/3 cup butter
2 tsp. vanilla

Melt butter and chocolate. Add the box of sugar a little at a time and stir into a smooth paste. Add cream a little at a time. Turn heat on simmer and stir while cooking. Cook approximately 5 minutes. While hot, drizzle over uncut pan of dessert.

Pralines

Ingredients:
1 cup white sugar
1 cup of dark brown sugar
1 cup of light brown sugar
1 cup of Pet Milk
1/3 stick of real butter
1 tsp. vanilla
1 1/2 cups of chopped pecans

Preparation:
1) Mix three cups of sugar and milk and bring to a boil over a medium flame until mixture reaches a soft ball stage.
2) Turn off heat and add butter and vanilla.
3) Beat with an electric mixer or by hand for about 3 minutes or until mixture glazes.
4) Add pecans and drop onto a wax sheet of paper or foil.
5) Let harden and wrap individually.

Fudge

2 cups sugar
1/2 cup cream or half and half
2, 1 oz. squares baking chocolate
1 Tbs. light Karo syrup
1 tsp. vanilla
1/4 cup butter
1 cup pecans (optional)

Preparation:
Put sugar, cream, chocolate and Karo syrup in a saucepan and cook, stirring constantly until it reaches softball stage. Remove from heat, add butter, let cool for 2 minutes and start beating rapidly. Add pecans and vanilla. Beat until glossy and pour into a buttered pan. Let cool and cut into squares.

March

Bella Luna Restaurant

Bella Luna is one of the country's most romantic restaurants with fabulous uncompromising views of the Mississippi River on one side as well as quaint French Quarter rooftops on the other. Chef Horst Pfeifer, co-owner and European Master Chef, is a native of Germany. His eclectic menu includes European and regional American influences with an emphasis on New Orleans favorites: house-made pastas, oven-roasted quail and sweet basil crusted redfish are just a few of the sumptuous delights. With wonderful food and an elegant living room, Glamour Magazine voted Bella Luna "one of the best places to kiss."

Karen and Horst Pfeifer not only run a beautiful restaurant, but donate their time to maintain an herb garden at the Ursuline Convent in the French Quarter.

Menu

Iced Imported Beer
Grand Marnier Margaritas
Papaya Iced Tea

Smoked Shrimp & Poblano Quesadillas *

Pico de Gallo with Serrano Peppers & Epazote *

Spicy Buffalo Chile with Black Beans and Blue Corn Tortilla Threads

Roasted Poblano Pepper Stuffed with Louisiana Seafood Served with Cilantro Pesto *

Steamed Maine Lobster Soft Taco with White Chocolate and Tomatillo Mole *

Tequila Flan with Fresh Pineapple and Strawberry Salsa

menu by Bella Luna Restaurant

White Chocolate Tomatillo Sauce with Cilantro and Corn
Serves 6

1 lb. tomatillos, peeled and cut in 1/2
3/4 cup diced onions
2 cloves garlic, peeled
2 fresh jalapeños, seeded
1 cup white corn
2 cups chicken stock
salt, pepper and cumin to your taste
1/4 cup white chocolate in chunks
1/2 bunch cilantro, finely chopped

Put everything but the chocolate and cilantro in a sauce pan over high heat. Once it begins to boil, lower the temperature to a simmer. Simmer 15 minutes, then add the white chocolate and cilantro to get a nice color. Simmer another 5-10 minutes. Remove from the heat and blend until smooth. Serve warm or at room temperature.

Steamed Maine Lobster Soft Taco with White Chocolate and Tomatillo Mole
Serves 6

18 flour tortillas, 6 inch
3 lobster, whole; steamed & shelled and cut into smaller pieces
3 Tbs. butter
1 medium onion, finely chopped
2 Tbs. sun-dried tomatoes
1/2 green bell pepper, finely chopped
1/2 red bell pepper, finely chopped
1 yellow bell pepper, finely chopped
1 Tbs. garlic, chopped
3 Tbs. sweet basil, finely chopped

salt and pepper to taste
Melt the butter in a pan then sauté the onion, sun-dried tomatoes and bell peppers until a light golden color. Now add the garlic and lobster. Sauté until everything is hot and add the basil. Season with salt and pepper.

Warm the tortillas by placing on burner for 10 seconds on each side.

Fill the tortillas with the lobster mixture, roll up like a soft taco and place on a plate with the tomatillo sauce and garnish with white cheddar and pico de gallo.

Pico de Gallo with Serrano Peppers and Epazote
Serves 6
1 bunch epazote*, finely chopped
1 large red onion, finely chopped
3 serrano peppers, finely chopped
1 lb. tomatoes, diced
3 limes, juice only
1/2 tsp. chopped garlic
Salt, pepper & cumin to taste

Mix all ingredients together, set for one hour and re-season to taste
* Cilantro may be substituted.

Roasted Poblano Pepper stuffed with Louisiana Seafood and topped with Cilantro Pesto
Serves 6

8 poblano peppers, washed

1 1/2 cups corn, cut off the cob
1/3 cup yellow onions
1/3 cup green onions
1 tsp. garlic

Sauté the above ingredients except peppers until wilted and let cool.

1/4 cup cilantro
1/3 cup cheddar cheese
1/3 cup mozzarella cheese
1/2 lb. crawfish tails
1/2 lb. crab meat
2 tsp. cumin
2 tsp. chili
salt and pepper to taste

Add the above ingredients to the cooled vegetable mixture.
Fry the 8 poblano peppers in peanut oil for three to five minutes until skins turn brown. Soak in ice water to cool. Peel peppers, slice open, remove seeds, and stuff with the above mixture. Cover peppers with batter (recipe follows).

1 cup flour
1/2 cup cornstarch
4 eggs, separated
1 cup milk

Beat flour, cornstarch, yolks and milk. With a mixer, whip whites until stiff, then fold into other ingredients.
Cover the peppers with batter.
Fry at 350° F for five minutes then bake at 450° F for 10 to 15 minutes.

Smoked Shrimp Quesadillas with Homemade Guacamole
Serves 6

Ingredients:
6 flour tortillas
2 Tbs. sundried tomatoes
3 Tbs. roasted, diced poblano peppers
6 Tbs. goat cheese
12 smoked shrimp
2 Tbs. minced herbs (coriander, Italian parsley)
6 Tbs. shredded mozzarella

Preparation:
1) Spread 1 tablespoon of goat cheese over each open tortilla.
2) Sprinkle 1 1/2 tablespoons of mozzarella over half of each tortilla.
3) Add peppers, shrimp (two on each tortilla), sundried tomatoes and herbs (one teaspoon per tortilla).
4) Add the remaining mozzarella (1 1/2 tablespoons on each tortilla).
5) Fold each tortilla in half.
6) Grill until the inside is hot and the outside is lightly browned and crisp.
7) Serve with homemade guacamole (see recipe).

Guacamole
Serves 6

Ingredients:
5 Avocados
1 Tbs. of cilantro
1 red bell pepper
3 limes
salt and pepper
2 jalapeño peppers
1 red onion
1 tomato
1 tsp. garlic
Cumin

Preparation:
1) Finely chop jalapeño, onions, tomato, bell peppers and cilantro.
2) Add ripe avocados to vegetables and mash with potato masher.
3) Add lime juice and seasonings. Let sit for one hour.

Brennan's Restaurant

A culinary phenomenon since 1946, Brennan's Restaurant has created some of the world's most famous and imaginative dishes such as Bananas Foster and Eggs Hussarde. Owen Edward Brennan, the founder of Brennan's Restaurant and creator of the legendary "Breakfast at Brennan's", was the culinary renaissance man of his time influencing the course of New Orleans gastronomy. Today Owen's sons Pip, Jimmy and Ted are the sole proprietors and continue to nurture the same standard of excellence in fine dining estabished by their father over 50 years ago.

Whether it's breakfast, lunch or dinner at Brennan's, you'll feel the history resounding through this historic French Quarter mansion. Guests dine in twelve dining rooms that surround a romantic patio with huge magnolia trees, lush foliage and a picturesque fountain.

Executive chef, Mike Roussel maintains Brennan's as a restaurant rich in the traditions of its past while exemplary in the trends of the present.

Menu

Brennan's Brandy Milk Punch *
Mimosas
Ramos Gin Fizz *
Chardonnay

Oyster Soup Brennan *
Grillades and Plantation Grits *
Garlic Bread and Cinnamon Toast *
Bananas Foster *

menu by Brennan's Restaurant

Brennan's Brandy Milk Punch

Ingredients for one cocktail:
1 cup ice cubes
1 1/2 oz. Napoleon brandy or bourbon
2 Tbs. simple syrup
1/2 cup half and half
3/4 tsp. vanilla
pinch of nutmeg

Combine all of the ingredients, except the nutmeg in a cocktail shaker. Shake vigorously, then pour into a chilled old-fashioned glass. Sprinkle with nutmeg and serve.

Ramos Gin Fizz

Ingredients for one cocktail:
1 1/2 oz. gin
1/4 tsp. orange flower water
1/8 tsp. vanilla
1/4 tsp. lemon juice
2 tsp. simple syrup
1 egg white
1/2 cup half and half
1/4 cup crushed ice

Combine all of the ingredients in a blender and blend for 15 seconds. Pour into a chilled old-fashioned glass and serve.

Oyster Soup Brennan
Serves 10-12

2 cups (about 48) shucked oysters
3 quarts cold water
3/4 cup (1 1/2 sticks) butter
1 cup celery, finely chopped
1 1/2 Tbs. garlic, finely chopped
1 cup scallions, finely chopped
4 bay leaves
1 Tbs. thyme leaves
1 cup all-purpose flour
1 1/2 Tbs. Worcestershire sauce
1 tsp. salt
1 tsp. white pepper
1/2 cup fresh parsley, finely chopped

Preparation:
1) In a large sauce pan, combine the oysters and 3 quarts cold water. Bring the water to a boil, then reduce the heat and simmer about 5 minutes skimming any residue from the surface.
2) Strain the oysters and reserve the stock. Dice the oysters and set aside.
3) Melt butter in a large pot and sauté the celery and garlic over medium heat for about 5 minutes until tender.

4) Add the scallions, bay leaves, and thyme, then stir in the flour. Cook the mixture for 5 minutes over low heat, stirring constantly.

5) Using a whisk, blend in the oyster stock, then add the Worcestershire sauce, salt, and pepper.

6) Cook the soup over medium heat about 20 minutes until thickened, then add the parsley and oysters. Simmer until the oysters are warmed through, about 5 minutes.

7) Remove the bay leaves before serving.

Grillades and Plantation Grits
Serves 8

Ingredients:
8 thinly pounded veal escalopes, about 3 oz. each
$1/2$ cup (1 stick) butter (Olive oil can be substituted)
$1/2$ cup olive oil
$1/2$ cup chopped onion
$1/2$ cup chopped scallions
3 garlic cloves, finely chopped
$1 1/2$ cups chopped green bell pepper
$1/2$ cup chopped celery
1 bay leaf
$1 1/2$ tsp. Italian seasoning
4 ripe tomatoes, diced
1 Tbs. Worcestershire sauce
2 Tbs. tomato paste
1 quart beef stock
2 Tbs. cornstarch
$1/4$ cup water
2 Tbs. chopped fresh parsley
Salt and black pepper
Plantation grits
Preheat oven to 175° F.

Preparation:
1) Season the veal escalopes on both sides with salt and pepper. Heat the butter in a large skillet and sauté the veal until lightly browned, about 3

minutes per side. Transfer the cooked meat to a platter and place in the warm oven while preparing the sauce.

2) Heat the olive oil in a large saucepan, then sauté the onions, scallions, garlic, bell pepper, and celery in the hot oil until tender. Stir in the bay leaf, Italian seasoning, tomatoes, Worcestershire, and tomato paste. When the mixture is well blended, add the beef stock and cook for 5 minutes, stirring frequently. In a small bowl, blend the cornstarch with $1/4$ cup water. Stir the liquid cornstarch into the sauce, then add the parsley. Season with salt and pepper to taste and cook over medium high heat until the sauce is reduced by about one fourth. Remove the bay leaves before serving.

3) Spoon the Grillade sauce onto eight plates and center a veal escalope on each. Place cooked grits on the side of the meat, ladle additional sauce over the veal and grits, and serve.

Plantation Grits
5 cups water
1 tsp. salt
1 cup grits
$1/4$ cup butter

In a medium saucepan, bring 5 cups water to a boil along with salt. Gradually add grits to the pan, stirring constantly. Reduce the heat and simmer the grits until thickened 5 to 10 min. Add the butter and stir until the butter is melted thoroughly. You could serve with shredded cheese on the top.

Garlic Bread
Serves 8

Ingredients:
3 small loaves French bread (about 12" long)
$1/2$ cup garlic butter
2 Tbs. paprika
3 Tbs. fresh parsley, finely chopped
$1/2$ cup freshly grated Parmesan cheese

Preparation:
(Preheat oven to 350° F.)
1) Split the loaves in half lengthwise.
2) Spread the garlic butter onto the cut side of each loaf.
3) Sprinkle with paprika and parsley, then transfer loaves to a baking sheet.
4) Bake in hot oven for 5 minutes, then sprinkle each slice with Parmesan cheese.
5) Bake an additional 3 minutes and cut each loaf diagonally, into 3 pieces. Serve warm.

Cinnamon Toast
Serves 6

Ingredients:
$1/4$ cup ($1/2$ stick) butter
2 small loaves of French bread (about 12" long)
1 tsp. cinnamon
1 tsp. sugar

Preparation:
(Preheat oven to 350° F.)
1) Split the loaves in half lengthwise. Spread a tablespoon of butter on the inside of each split loaf of bread.
2) Combine the cinnamon and sugar and sprinkle the mixture over the butter.
3) Spread the pieces butter side up, on a baking sheet.
4) Broil for 3-4 minutes until golden brown. Serve warm.

Bananas Foster
Serves 4

Ingredients:
1/4 cup (1/2 stick) butter
1 cup brown sugar
1/2 tsp. cinnamon
1/4 cup banana liqueur
4 bananas, cut in half lengthwise,
then halved
1/4 cup dark rum
4 scoops vanilla ice cream

Preparation:
1) Combine the butter, sugar, and cinnamon in a flambé pan or skillet.
2) Place the pan over low heat either on an alcohol burner or on the top of the stove, and cook, stirring until the sugar dissolves.
3) Stir in the banana liqueur, then place the bananas in the pan. When the banana sections soften and begin to brown, carefully add the rum.
4) Continue to cook the sauce until the rum is hot, then tip the pan slightly to ignite the rum.
5) When the flames subside, lift the bananas out of the pan and place four pieces over each portion of ice cream.
6) Generously spoon warm sauce over the top of the ice cream and serve immediately.

Mr. B's Bistro

Since 1979, Mr. B's on Royal Street in the French Quarter has proudly offered their style of Creole cuisine; a mixture of French, Spanish, Italian, African, American Indian and Caribbean influences utilizing the finest foods of Southern Louisiana. Chef Michelle McRaney, and the Brennan family bring their patrons creative simple and honest food in a cozy bistro style. Whether you are there for a business lunch, with friends and family for dinner or their delightful jazz brunch, you'll enjoy innovative culinary creations and impeccable service. Soft, upbeat piano music will have you tapping your toes while you savor your next incredible dinner at Mr. B's.

Strawberry Pear Cocktails
Serves 6

Ingredients:
4 cups fresh ripe strawberries, hulled and halved
2 ripe pears, peeled, cored and sliced
1 cup plain yogurt
1/2 cup fresh orange juice
mint leaves and additional strawberries for garnish

Preparation:
1) Combine strawberries, pears, yogurt, and orange juice in a blender and process until smooth.
2) Garnish with fresh mint leaves and strawberries.

Menu

Chilled Chardonnay
Mimosas
Strawberry Pear Cocktails *

Crabmeat Salad on French Bread
Croutons *
Soft Shell Crabs with Almonds and
Shallot Dill Vinaigrette *

Strawberry Shortcake *

menu by Mr. B's Bistro

Crabmeat Salad on French Bread Croutons
Serves 8

Ingredients:
1 lb. jumbo lump crab meat
1/4 cup minced shallots
2 Tbs. minced celery
2 Tbs. minced red bell pepper
3/4 cup mayonnaise
1 tsp. Crystal hot sauce
2 tsp. lemon juice
1 tsp. Creole mustard

Preparation:
1) Mix all the ingredients together.
2) Serve atop sliced French bread croutons.

Croutons:
1 loaf French bread

Cut bread into 1/2" rounds. Lightly toast rounds (butter or margarine optional). Let cool and spoon salad on top to serve.

Soft Shell Crab with Almonds and Shallot Dill Vinaigrette
Serves 6

Ingredients:
4 Tbs. chopped shallots
1/4 cup chopped fresh dill
1/4 cup corn oil
2 Tbs. extra virgin olive oil
1 tsp. lemon juice
1 tsp. lemon zest
1 tsp. rice wine vinegar
6 soft shell crabs, cleaned
1/4 cup all-purpose flour
1 tsp. salt
1 tsp. black pepper
1 egg
1 Tbs. milk
1/2 cup sliced almonds, toasted, and chopped
3 Tbs. clarified butter
3 cups fresh baby greens

Preparation:
1) In a bowl, whisk together shallots, dill, corn oil, olive oil, lemon juice, lemon zest, and rice wine vinegar. Set aside.
2) Combine the flour, salt, and pepper in a small bowl.
3) Whisk egg and milk in another small bowl.
4) Add toasted, chopped almonds to a third bowl.
5) Dredge each crab in the flour, then the egg mixture, and finally the almonds.
6) Add the crabs and sauté over medium heat for 3 or 4 minutes on each side.

7) Divide the baby greens among 6 plates and place a crab atop the greens. Spoon on the vinaigrette and serve.

Strawberry Shortcake
Serves 10

Shortcake Biscuit Ingredients:
2 cups all-purpose flour
1 tsp. salt
1 Tbs. double-acting baking powder
2 tsp. granulated sugar
3/4 to 1 cup heavy cream
melted butter

Preparation:
1) Sift the dry ingredients together and fold in the heavy cream until it makes a soft dough that can be easily handled.
2) Turn out on a floured board, knead for about 1 minute, and then pat to a thickness of about 3/4 inch.
3) Cut in rounds, dip in melted butter, and arrange on a baking sheet. Bake in a preheated 425° F oven for 15 to 18 minutes.

Filling Ingredients:
7 cups fresh ripe strawberries, hulled and halved
1 cup granulated sugar
2 Tbs. balsamic vinegar
juice of 2 lemons

Preparation:
1) Combine all of the above ingredients.
2) Split shortcake biscuits in half. Put the bottoms on plates.
3) Divide the strawberry filling among the plates. Add a little whipped cream and top the biscuits.

Galatoire's Restaurant

Galatoire's Restaurant located on Bourbon Street in New Orleans has been a landmark since 1905. It has been owned and operated by family members for four generations and prides itself on serving consistently top quality French Creole food without bowing to "boutique trends." Oysters Rockefeller, crabmeat Maison, eggs sardou and shrimp remoulade are some of their signature dishes.

Reservations are accepted only on Tuesday, Wednesday, and Thursday and for 8 or more, otherwise it's first come, first served. They just started taking credit cards! Waiters in tuxes, ceiling fans reflected in mirrored walls and white linen table cloths and napkins all remind you of France, but only in New Orleans will you find the dining experience called Galatoire's!

Shrimp Remoulade
Serves 8

Ingredients:
1 bunch parsley, stems removed
2 ribs celery
2 cloves garlic
1 Tbs. minced bell pepper
1 cup Creole mustard
4 Tbs. paprika
2 Tbs. prepared horseradish
1 cup red wine vinegar
1 tsp. Tabasco sauce
1 tsp. Worcestershire sauce
salt to taste
1/4 tsp. black pepper
Pinch cayenne pepper
1 pt. salad oil
4 cups shredded lettuce
2 lb. shrimp, boiled and peeled
2 lemons, quartered

Preparation:
1) Using a food processor, chop the parsley, celery, garlic, and bell pepper to a coarse puree and transfer into a large mixing bowl.
2) Add the mustard, paprika, horseradish, vinegar, Tabasco, Worcestershire sauce, salt, black pepper, and cayenne pepper.
3) Using a wire whisk, beat constantly, adding small amounts of oil at a dribble until the sauce achieves a smooth consistency.
4) Transfer to a refrigerator to marinate for 24 hours.
5) To serve: place small amounts of shredded lettuce onto each chilled salad plate. Place equal amounts of shrimp over lettuce. Stir sauce and spoon over shrimp. Garnish with lemon wedges.

Crawfish Salad
Serves 8

Ingredients:
2 heads romaine lettuce
2 lbs. crawfish tails
1/2 cup mayonnaise
4 tsp. Creole mustard
4 Tbs. lemon juice
2 oz. white wine
8 finely chopped green onions
4 tsp. finely chopped parsley
4 tsp. capers
2 lemons, quartered
black pepper to taste

Preparation:
1) Cut the stalk ends from the lettuce. Discard outermost leaves and select four young tender ones for the salad bed. Soak leaves in ice water for 5 minutes, then pat dry.

menu

Veuve Clicquot Champagne
Galatoire's Special Cocktails

Shrimp Remoulade *
Potatoes Brabant
Crawfish Salad *
Godchaux Salad *

Crepes Maison with Triple Sec *

menu by Galatoire's

2) In a mixing bowl, combine crawfish tails, mayonnaise, mustard, lemon juice, wine, green onions, parsley, capers, and pepper. Simply mix together well and chill.
3) To serve, place a lettuce leaf on each chilled salad plate. Spoon equal amounts of mixture onto each bed. Garnish with a lemon wedge.
(For our June party, we put all salads in colorful Chinese containers.)

Godchaux Salad
Serves 6-8

1 head iceberg lettuce, cored and cubed
2 large tomatoes, stems removed and cubed
1 lb. backfin lump crabmeat
30 - 35 large shrimp, boiled and peeled
2/3 cup salad oil
1/3 cup red wine vinegar
1/2 cup Creole mustard
3 hard boiled eggs
12 anchovies

    In a large bowl, combine the lettuce, tomatoes, crabmeat and shrimp. In a small bowl, combine the oil, vinegar, and mustard and mix well with a wire whisk. Pour the dressing over the salad and toss.
    Divide the salad onto 6 chilled plates. Garnish each salad with 1/2 of a sieved hard boiled egg and 2 anchovies.

Crepes Maison
2 crepes per person, serves 6-8

Crepe Batter Ingredients:
3/4 cup flour
2 tsp. sugar
1/2 tsp. salt
3 eggs
3/4 cup milk
1 Tbs. butter

Crepe Preparation:
1) Sift the flour, sugar, and salt together in a bowl.
2) In a small mixing bowl, beat the eggs.
3) Add the milk and the dry ingredients and beat the batter in a mixer on medium speed or blend in a blender until the batter is smooth.

4) Allow the batter to sit for about 1 hour before cooking.
5) Heat a 6 inch crepe pan over medium high heat.
6) Lift the pan and brush the bottom of the pan lightly with melted butter.
7) Pre-measure 2 Tbs. of batter, and pour the batter in the middle of the pan. Quickly tilt the pan so that the batter spreads evenly over the bottom.
8) Return the pan to the heat, and brown the crepe lightly on both sides.
9) Repeat the above process until all the batter is used and place finished crepes between layers of wax paper until they are ready to fill.

Crepe Filling Ingredients:
12 Tbs. (6 oz.) currant jelly
1/2 cup sliced almonds
1/4 cup Triple Sec Liqueur
3 Tbs. sifted powdered sugar

Garnish:
Very thin slivers of orange and lemon

Crepe Filling Preparation:
1) Spread 1 Tbs. of jelly on each crepe and fold the crepe into thirds.
2) Place them side by side in an oblong baking pan and sprinkle the crepes with sliced almonds and add slivers of oranges and lemons sparsely on top.
3) Place the crepes under a broiler for 3-5 minutes or until the almonds are lightly toasted.
4) Remove the crepes from the broiler and sprinkle with Triple Sec Liqueur and powdered sugar.

Dooky Chase Restaurant

Rich in tradition, Dooky Chase Restaurant features authentic Creole cooking, "soul-food" style. Leah and Dooky Chase have created an elegant restaurant adorned with an exquisite collection of Afro-American art. This colorful private collection of art is matched by Mrs. Chase's colorful Creole dishes: gumbo, shrimp Clemenceau, bread pudding with whiskey sauce and many more.

Mrs. Chase has gained local and national attention for her generous contribution of talent, service and time to numerous organizations. She was featured in "I Dream a World: Portraits of Black Women Who Changed America," and received the National Candace Award in 1984 as one of the ten most outstanding black women in America.

Stuffed Po-Boy
Serves 10

1 large loaf French bread or submarine sandwich bread
2 lbs. (sliced) good smoked ham
1 lb. Monterey jack cheese with hot peppers
1/2 cup dill relish (drained well)
1/2 cup mayonnaise
2 Tbs. yellow mustard

Menu

Freshly Squeezed Lemonade
Soft Drinks, Beer and Minted Iced Tea

Sweet Potato Rolls
Stuffed Po-Boy or Submarine Sandwich*
Midori Melon Bowl *
Curry Chicken Salad *

Hand-cranked Ice Cream
Mini Desserts:
Old-Fashioned Bread Pudding with Bourbon Sauce
Fruit and Pecan Tarts

menu by Dooky Chase Restaurant

Chop ham and cheese. Place in bowl and add relish, mayonnaise and mustard. Mix well. Cut bread in half. Remove center of bread. Stuff ham and cheese in each half of bread. Chill for 1/2 hour to 45 minutes. Place halves together on tray. Garnish with parsley, cherry tomatoes, green and black olives. Cut into 2" slices and serve.

Midori Melon Bowl
Serves 15

1 watermelon
2 cantaloupes
2 cups Midori (Melon Liqueur)

Experiment with whole melon to find most stable sitting position, and cut the top off just above the halfway point. Scoop out and remove seeds to make a watermelon bowl. Keep, cube and pit the watermelon. Cut and remove seeds and rind from cantaloupes. Cube and set aside. Place cantaloupe and watermelon together in watermelon bowl. Pour Midori over top. Chill for 1 hour. Garnish with mint leaves and serve.

Curry Chicken Salad
Serves 8

4 lbs. cooked chicken meat (diced)
2 cups chopped celery
2 Tbs. curry powder
1 1/2 cups mayonnaise
1 Tbs. Lawry's seasoned salt
1 cup diced red apples, unpeeled
2 cups green seedless grapes
3 Tbs. chopped parsley

Place chicken in large bowl and add remaining ingredients. Toss well. Arrange on lettuce leaves and garnish with fresh strawberries.

Old-Fashioned Bread Pudding with Bourbon Sauce
Serves 8

1 loaf stale French bread
(or 5 cups cubed stale white bread)
2, 12 oz. cans evaporated milk
1 cup water
6 eggs, beaten
8 oz. crushed pineapple
1 large apple, grated
1 cup raisins
1 1/2 cups sugar
5 Tbs. vanilla
1/4 lb. butter, softened

In a bowl, break bread and moisten with evaporated milk and water. Pour eggs over mixture and mix well. Add pineapple, apple, raisins, sugar, and vanilla and mix well. Cut butter into pieces and add to mixture, mixing all ingredients well. Pour into a greased 9" X 13" baking dish. Bake at 350° F for 30 to 40 minutes. Can be served with ice cream or bourbon sauce.

Bourbon Sauce
Makes 1 1/2 cups

3 Tbs. butter
1 Tbs. flour
1/2 cup sugar
1 cup cream
1 Tbs. vanilla
1 tsp. nutmeg
1 oz. bourbon

In a small saucepan, melt butter and flour and cook for 5 minutes. Stir in sugar; add cream. Cook for 3 minutes. Add vanilla, nutmeg, and bourbon. Let simmer for 5 minutes.

Antoine's Restaurant

World famous Antoine's Restaurant on Saint Louis Street in the French Quarter opened its doors in 1840 and has had 5 continuous generations of the Alciatore-Guste family as owners and proprietors. Steeped in tradition, the dining rooms and special private rooms like the Rex Room, Proteus Room, Escargot Room, 1840 Room, etc., make the Antoine's experience totally unique.

At Antoine's your waiter guides you to the most fresh and available selections beginning with appetizers like Oysters Rockefeller or Crabmeat Ravigote then a fish or meat course and perhaps their famous Baked Alaska. The wine cellar is world renowned. The elegant and comfortable atmosphere and relationship of clients to waiters, as well as the generations of families; customers, workers and owners have all contributed to the continued existence and operation of Antoine's, now under the leadership of Mr. Bernard Guste.

Lobster Thermidor
Serves 40

15 lb. of steamed lobster meat (6 oz. per person)
2.5 quarts of sherry wine
1.3 gallons of béchamel sauce
5 Tbs. lobster base
16 oz. melted butter
salt and white pepper to taste

1 lb. grated Swiss cheese
1 lb. grated romano cheese
1 lb. grated mozzarella
28 oz. bread crumbs
(mix these ingredients together for cheese topping)

Menu

Appetizers & Drinks on the Beach:

Champagne
Antoine's Smiles
Piña Colada
Frozen Peach Daiquiri
Prosciutto with Papaya
Shrimp Ravigote with Avocado *
Artichokes Aioli *
Display of Smoked Favorites: Sausage, Pork
Tenderloin and Baby Back Ribs with Hot Honey Dip

At the Table:

Chardonnay
Chilled Breadfruit Vichyssoise
Crayfish Timbale on a Bed of Exotic Greens
with Hearts of Palm *
Lobster Thermidor *

Pineapple and Banana Flambé with Vanilla Ice Cream
Café au Lait, Expresso, Cognac and Cigars

menu by Antoine's Restaurant

Cut the lobster meat into 1 inch pieces. Sauté meat with butter slightly, then add sherry that has been reduced by 1/3 and lobster base. Then add béchamel sauce. Add salt and pepper to taste. Spoon the mixture into ramekins. Top each ramekin with cheese mixture and place in a 375° F oven until brown.

Béchamel Sauce

1.2 gallons of milk
20 oz. of butter
20 oz. of plain flour
20 egg yolks

Melt the butter in a sauce pan and stir in flour. Cook the roux over medium heat until it turns slightly golden in color. Warm milk, then add the roux. Cook sauce to thicken, remove from heat. Let cool slightly, then add egg yolk, while stirring vigorously, and set aside.

Crayfish Timbale on a Bed of Exotic Greens with Hearts of Palm
Serves 40

1 1/2 gallon of hot fish stock
24 oz. of unflavored gelatin
(whip together and cool slightly)
32 oz. Antoine's mayonnaise
juice of two lemons
5 lbs. chopped crayfish tails
salt and white pepper to taste

4 bunches of green onions, finely chopped
1 medium white onion, finely chopped
2 bell peppers, finely chopped
1 bunch parsley, finely chopped

In a large chase bowl, put mayonnaise, juice, chopped mixture, crayfish tails, and salt and pepper to taste and mix well. Then pour gelatin fish stock, a little at a time while stirring. Check for seasoning. Spoon the Timbale into ramekins, and refrigerate over night. To serve, unmold onto a bed of exotic greens. Add hearts of palm on the side.

Antoine's Mayonnaise
6 egg yolks
1 1/2 pinch salt and white pepper
1 1/2 splashes of white vinegar and lemon juice
20 oz. Wesson oil

Beat yolks on high till the mixture is thick and light in color (off white). Add salt, pepper, vinegar, and lemon juice. Beat mixture for one minute. Put mixer on low, then add oil a little at a time, not too fast until the oil is all in. Now beat on high for 1 1/2 minutes. Chill and it is ready.

Aioli Sauce
(To be used as a sauce with steamed artichokes)
Yields 8 oz.

8 oz. Antoine's mayonnaise
1 Tbs. pureed garlic

Mix mayonnaise and garlic with hand whip.

Shrimp Ravigote
Serves 40

10 lbs. raw, headless shrimp (boiled and peeled)
3 Tbs. minced bell pepper
3 Tbs. minced green onions
3 Tbs. minced anchovies
3 Tbs. minced pimento
4 cups Antoine's mayonnaise

Mix with chilled mayonnaise to make the sauce. Mix the sauce and shrimp together. Serve with slices of avocado.

Remoulade Sauce

Yields 28 oz.

16 oz. catsup
6 drops of Tabasco
6 oz. Lea and Perrins Worcestershire sauce
9 oz. Creole mustard
3 oz. vinaigrette
2 Tbs. horse radish
1 Tbs. minced green onion
1 Tbs. minced celery
1 Tbs. minced parsley

Mix very well with a hand whip.

Mike's On The Avenue

Vicky Bayley and famed chef and artist Mike Fennelly have created a sophisticated, artistic restaurant with a cuisine that is a blend of Southwestern, Asian and Creole influences. There are "no holds barred" in Chef Mike Fennelly's kitchen. Every dinner plate at Mike's is a visual delight. Vicky and Mike have brought a brilliant style of cooking to New Orleans. Located on Saint Charles Avenue downtown, Mike's On The Avenue offers a modern American cross-cultural experience.

Mike's is "the place" to be seen for lunch, dinner or one of their special theme nights in which the restaurant is transformed by Mike's painted backdrops and flower arrangements. Unique menus are featured on theme nights for "A Night in Havana," "A Night in Casablanca," and more…

The restaurant has consistently been chosen as one of the top best restaurants in New Orleans by *Food and Wine*, *Zagats*, *Gourmet* and *Conde Nast*.

Mike's on the Avenue has changed hands, but Executive chef Mike Fennelly and chef Scott Serpas present some of their favorites for this special dinner.

Chipolte Caesar Dressing

1 - 1 1/2 oz. anchovies (drained and rinsed)
2 Tbs. roasted garlic
2 egg yolks
2 small limes (juice of)
1 Tbs. Dijon mustard
2-3 chipoltes in adobe
1 large shallot

Menu

Pouilly-Fuissé:
Crawfish Spring Rolls
Barbecued Oysters with Pancetta
Roasted Chicken and Corn Quesadillas with
Saffron Creme Fraiche

Fumé Blanc
Chipolte Caesar Salad *
Crab Cakes served with Ancho Chili Mayonaise
and Salsa Fresca *

Port Wine
Crème Brûlée *

menu by Mike's on the Avenue

1/2 tsp. cumin
1 1/2 cups salad or canola oil
1/2 cups olive oil
3/4 tsp. salt

Place all ingredients in food processor except oils. Puree for 2 to 3 minutes. Scrape down bowl; turn machine back on and slowly pour oil in thin stream. Should resemble mayonnaise like consistency. Toss with Romaine lettuce leaves, homemade garlic croutons and slices of parmesan cheese.

Crab Cakes with Ancho Chili Mayonaise and Salsa Fresca

1¼ lbs. crab meat
1 large jalapeño - grilled, skinned, and seeded
2 Tbs. cilantro
¾ cup mayonnaise
¾ cup onions, minced
½ bunch green onions
1 large garlic clove, minced
½ cup bread crumbs
2 Tbs. chives
3 tsp. parsley
1 tsp. salt

Lightly rub jalapeño with oil and season. Grill pepper until blistered. Skin and seed pepper. Add jalapeño and cilantro to food processor and mix for 1 minute. Add mayonnaise and mix for 2 minutes. Add crabmeat and remaining ingredients and form into 2 oz. cakes. Dust with additional flour, buttermilk, and bread crumbs. Cook on lightly greased grill until brown. Serve 2 cakes per person.

Ancho Chili Sauce (to be used in ancho chili mayo.)

Ingredients:
1½ roasted red peppers, peeled and seeded
3 lightly grilled ancho chilis, seeded
3 grilled tomatoes
1 small red onion, grilled
1 cup tomato juice
1 Tbs. minced garlic
½ Tbs. toasted coriander, cumin and Szechwan pepper
1 tsp. salt
½ tsp. pepper
Juice of 1 lemon

Combine all ingredients and simmer for 1½ hours. Blend in food processor until smooth.

Ancho Chili Mayonnaise

Ingredients:
1 egg
6 egg yolks
3 Tbs. Ancho Chili Sauce
4 Tbs. lime juice
2 tsp. Dijon mustard
4 tsp. chimayo chile
4 tsp. balsamic vinegar
1 tsp. salt
1 tsp. black pepper
1 tsp. chopped garlic
1 tsp. ground cumin
3 cups olive oil

Combine all ingredients except olive oil in the bowl of your food processor and blend until combined. With processor still running, slowly drizzle in the oil until blended.

Mike's serves the crab cakes on a bed of baby greens with honey mustard vinaigrette. Artfully placed on the plate are the ancho chili mayonnaise, salsa fresca, guacamole and Mike's own homemade potato chips.

Crème Brûlée
Serves 12

4 cups heavy cream
1 cup sugar
½ vanilla bean
4 egg yolks

Topping:
raw sugar (available at health food stores)
or
mix of half light brown/half white granulated sugar

Bring cream, sugar, and vanilla just to a boil. Add beaten eggs slowly while whisking, into the mixture. Strain mixture and pour into oven proof cups. Put cups in a pan with hot water half way up the sides of the cups. Cover with foil and bake at 300° F until the center is set. Chill thoroughly. Lightly sprinkle the tops with the raw sugar and brown it to a golden color by applying a blowtorch flame with a light and even motion over the top. If you prefer, you can put the cups (on a metal tray) into your oven broiler for a few minutes on high. Watch closely and turn the tray if browning is uneven. Serve promptly.

Joel's Grand Cuisine

Whether it's his restaurant in Covington, Louisiana (just outside New Orleans) or his exquisitely catered events, Joel Dondis has as his goal to create great food with the best products, beautifully presented, with excellent service that's reflective of the client he serves. Kodak, Hallmark and General Electric are just a few clients that come to him to cater events from 2 to 2500 people. Beginning his culinary sojourn at the age of 11, he later studied in Europe, worked with Emeril Lagasse for 3 years and now presides over his own catering business.

Joel is taking New Orleans by storm with his new project, a state-of-the-art catering facility including designer in-house wares and a tasting showroom where clients can experience the full spectrum of Joel's Grand Cuisine.

Zucchini Basil Muffins
Makes 2 dozen

Ingredients:
2 large eggs, room temperature
3/4 cup milk
2/3 cup canola oil
2 1/2 cups unbleached flour
1/4 cup sugar
1 Tbs. baking powder
2 tsp. salt
2 cups zucchini, shredded but not peeled
2 Tbs. minced fresh basil
1/2 cup grated parmesan cheese

Menu

Sauvignon Blanc and Pinot Noir

Petite Acorn Squash Cakes topped with Brown Sugar and Aged Stilton Cheese, served warm, accented by Harvest Fresh Carved Gourds

Apple Cider Champagne Cocktail

Basil-Zucchini Muffins flavored with Parmesan Cheese * and Pumpkin-Pecan Muffins, both served with Honey Butter *

Raddichio, Watercress, Leaf Spinach and Arugula Salad Tossed with a Toasted Walnut and Sundried Cherry Vinaigrette

Oven Roasted Semi-Boneless Quail filled with Savory Chicken Stuffing, studded with Roasted Bell Peppers, French Shallots, Fresh Thyme and Crispy Bacon *

Sweet Onion Tart *

Pumpkin Caramel Custard with Candied Pumpkin and Praline Creme Anglaise *

menu by Joel's Grand Cuisine

Preparation:
1) Preheat oven to 425° F.
2) In a large bowl, beat the eggs. Add the milk and oil. Mix well.
3) In a separate bowl, blend flour, sugar, baking powder and salt.
4) Add flour mixture to egg mixture one cup at a time and stir until thick.
5) Gently stir in shredded zucchini and basil until mixed well.
6) Pour into large greased (or teflon) muffin pans. Sprinkle parmesan on

top of each muffin.
7) Bake for 20 to 22 minutes (or 15 minutes if cups are small).

Honey Butter

Ingredients:
1 lb. softened butter
4 oz. grade A pure clover honey

Preparation:
Blend butter and honey together in mixer. Do not overmix.

Oven Roasted Semi-Boneless Quail
Serves 6

6 partially deboned quail
2 slices sourdough bread
3/4 cup milk
1 egg
8 slices bacon
1 tsp. thyme
3 Tbs. shallot, peeled and diced
1 red bell pepper, diced
1/4 tsp. ground cayenne pepper
1 lb. boneless, uncooked skinless chicken breast, diced
1 Tbs. brandy

Preparation:
1) Preheat oven to 400° F.
2) Sauté shallots until transparent, stir in the brandy and set aside.
3) Sauté bacon until crispy, drain and set aside.
4) Mix sourdough bread and milk together in a bowl. Drain the milk

out of the bowl, then squeeze excess milk out of the bread.

5) Put chicken, egg, red pepper, and sourdough bread in a food processor and pulse. Do not grind too much.

6) Place the mixture in a bowl and add all of the ingredients except the quail. Mix well and refrigerate for 2 hours.

7) Place the breast side of the quail down. Cut a slit in the skin of the back and open. Season with salt and pepper.

8) Make 3 oz. balls out of the mixture and place a ball in each quail. Flip the quail over and shape it with your hands until rounded.

9) Bake on a sheet pan covered with parchment paper in an oven preheated to 400° F. Cook for about 20 minutes, or until a meat thermometer placed in the center of the quail reads 150° F, or when the juice runs clear.

Sweet Onion Tart
Serves 12

Ingredients:
2 sheets of puff pastry dough
2 large cloves of garlic, peeled
4 medium red onions, peeled and sliced in 1/2" rounds
4 Tbs. oil (blend of 80% canola and 20% olive)
2 tsp. fresh whole leaf thyme, finely chopped
1 tsp. fresh rosemary, finely chopped
1/2 tsp. salt
1/2 tsp. ground black pepper
4 large eggs
1 cup heavy cream
1 Tbs. Crystal hot sauce
2/3 cup grated parmesan cheese

Preparation:
1) Preheat oven to 425° F. Lightly grease two 9" pie pans. Place a puff pastry dough sheet in each pan and trim to the edge. Refrigerate until ready to use.

2) Coat sliced onions and garlic with olive oil mixture. Place onions on oven-proof rack and roast for 20 minutes. Place garlic on rack with onions and roast for an additional 20 minutes.

3) Chop the roasted garlic.

4) In a medium size mixing bowl, mix eggs, cream, herbs, salt, pepper and hot sauce with wire whisk until thoroughly blended. Add chopped roasted garlic.

5) Layer the roasted onion slices on the bottom of the prepared pie pans. Cover onion slices with the egg mixture.

6) Sprinkle with parmesan.

7) Bake at 425° F. for 25 to 30 minutes on bottom rack of oven. Cool slightly before slicing.

Pumpkin Caramel Custard
Serves 12

Ingredients:
11 large eggs (6 whole, 5 yolks only)
3 cups milk
2 tsp. pure vanilla extract
3/4 tsp. salt
3/4 cup pumpkin
2 cups sugar
2 Tbs. ginger powder
1 1/2 tsp. nutmeg
1 1/2 tsp. ground cinnamon
1/8 tsp. ground cloves
4 Tbs. water

Preparation:
1) Preheat oven to 350° F. Arrange an oven rack just below the center. Grease twelve 6 to 8 oz. custard cups.

2) Vigorously whisk the eggs, egg yolks, and vanilla in a large mixing bowl until blended. Set aside.

3) Place the milk, pumpkin, one cup of sugar, spices and salt in a medium saucepan and put it to the side.

4) Put the other cup of sugar and the water in a saucepan and boil over medium heat without stirring. Swirl the pan the moment it starts boiling and continue to swirl over the heat until the mixture turns a rich amber color, about 4 to 5 minutes.

5) Remove the caramel from the heat and immediately pour it into the custard cups. Make sure the bottoms of the cups are evenly coated. Place the cups in a shallow baking pan and pour enough hot water in the pan to come two-thirds of the way up the cups. Set aside.

6) Bring the pumpkin mixture just to a boil over medium heat. Whisk vigorously. While whisking, pour the pumpkin mixture into the egg mixture. Strain.

7) Pour the pumpkin-egg mixture into the custard cups and place them, with the baking pan, in the oven. Reduce heat to 325° F and bake until custards are firm, about 1 hour and 15 minutes. To test the firmness, insert a tester close to, but not in the center of a custard until the tester comes out clean.

8) Remove the custard cups from the water bath. Cool on a rack then refrigerate for 4 to 6 hours or overnight.

9) When ready to serve, run a thin knife along the edges of each custard cup and invert onto serving dishes. Top the custard with the praline whipped cream and sprinkle with toasted pecans.

Praline Whipped Cream
Makes 1 quart

Ingredients:
3/4 cup pecan halves
2 cups heavy cream
4 Tbs. sugar
4 Tbs. praline liqueur

Preparation:
1) In a mixer, whip the cream and the sugar to a medium soft peak. Whip in the praline liqueur.
2) Put the whipped cream on each pumpkin caramel custard and sprinkle the pecans on top.

Commander's Palace

Commander's Palace, nestled in the middle of the garden district has been a New Orleans landmark since 1880. Owners Ella, Dottie, Dick and John Brennan have created the Commander's atmosphere. Lally Brennan, Dickie Brennan and Brad Brennan Bridgeman help with the day-to-day operations. When you go to lunch, dinner or their famous jazz brunch, it's like a well-run party given by old friends - with great flowers, conviviality, fun and splendid wines and food.

The mixture of Creole, American and Commander's own creations under the guidance of executive chef, Jamie Shannon, have propelled Commander's into the 90's with fresh and new ideas for its famous haute Creole cuisine. Under Jamie's leadership, Commander's has received several honors: Chef of the Year 1992, *Food and Wine Magazine's* Number One Restaurant in America for 1995, "96 and "97 and *Zagat Survey's* Most Popular Restaurant in1996. Jamie's a real sportsman and has created his favorites for us!

Menu

White Burgundy
Golden Roasted Oysters with Artichokes, Garlic and Parmesan Cheese*

Speckled Belly Goose Gumbo & Alligator Sausage over Rice and Chiffonade of Green Onions *

Pinot Noir or Zinfandel
Roast Rack of Venison *
Wild Mushroom and Four Bean Salad*

Champagne or Sauterne
Fig Tart *

menu by Commander's Palace

Golden Roasted Oysters
Serves 8

Ingredients:
6 large artichokes, stems trimmed
2 Tbs. olive oil, plus more for drizzling
1 Tbs. minced garlic
salt and freshly ground pepper
2 Tbs. fresh lemon juice
2 tsp. fresh oregano
4 cups fresh bread crumbs (from about two baguettes)
1/4 cup freshly grated Parmesan cheese
1/4 cup minced fresh flat-leaf parsley
2 Tbs. unsalted butter, melted
4 dozen freshly shucked large oysters on the half shell
kosher salt, for the platters
sweet paprika, for dusting
lemon wedges and Louisiana hot sauce

Preparation:

1) Arrange the artichokes in a large steaming basket, stem ends down. Set the basket in a large pot with 2 inches of water. Cover and bring to a boil over high heat. Reduce the heat to moderate and steam the artichokes until tender when pierced with a knife (about 25 minutes). Transfer to a platter. When cool enough to handle, remove the artichoke leaves. Using a teaspoon, scrape out the hairy chokes. Cut each artichoke bottom into 7 slices, then cut the large center slices in half.

2) In a non reactive skillet, warm 1 Tbs. of olive oil over moderate heat. Add the garlic and cook until fragrant, about 1 minute. Add the artichoke slices, season with salt and pepper and cook, stirring, until lightly browned, about 4 minutes. Add the lemon juice and oregano and stir gently. Remove from the heat and add the remaining 1 Tbs. of olive oil.

3) In a large bowl, mix the bread crumbs with the Parmesan, parsley, $3/4$ tsp. salt, $1/4$ tsp. pepper and the butter.

(MAKE AHEAD: The artichokes and the seasoned bread crumbs can be refrigerated separately for up to 1 day.)

4) Preheat the oven to 450° F. Set the oysters in their shells on large baking sheets, fitting them snugly to prevent tilting. Put 1 artichoke slice and a pinch of the cooked garlic on each oyster, drizzle with olive oil and mount a scant 2 Tbs. of the bread crumbs on top.

5) Roast the oysters in the upper third of the oven for about 10 minutes, or until golden brown and bubbling. Meanwhile, cover serving platters with a layer of kosher salt. Sprinkle the roasted oysters with paprika and set them on the salt. Serve immediately, with lemon wedges and hot sauce.

Roast Rack of Venison
Serves 8

Ingredients:
1 5lb. rack of venison
1 clove fresh garlic, peeled
cracked black pepper
kosher salt
1 Tbs. rosemary, fresh
1 Tbs. thyme, fresh
1 Tbs. oregano, fresh
1 Tbs. basil, fresh
2 bay leaves
$1 1/2$ cups Cabernet Sauvignon
$1/4$ cup French shallots
1 diced tomato
3 cups light veal stock (or chicken stock)
2 Tbs. cold butter

Preparation:
1) Season the rack with fresh garlic, cracked black pepper and kosher salt. Rub with fresh herbs of rosemary, thyme, oregano, and basil. Let marinate overnight.
2) In a medium skillet pan sear for 10 minutes then place in a 350 F oven for 20 minutes, until medium rare. Pull out and let rest.

Venison Reduction Sauce
3) De glaze the sauté pan with cabernet, cut French shallots, diced tomato, and bay leaves. Simmer for about 5 minutes.
4) Add the venison stock and reduce by half. Add the cold butter to finish the sauce. Strain and set aside.

Wild Mushroom and Four Bean Salad
Serves 8

Ingredients:
$1/2$ cup roasted wild mushrooms, seasoned
$1/4$ cup julienne sweet onions, cooked
$1/4$ cup field peas, cooked
$1/4$ cup red beans, cooked
$1/4$ cup white beans, cooked
$1/4$ cup black beans, cooked
$1/2$ pound baby greens, cooked
1 oz. cane vinaigrette - two parts olive oil, one part cane vinegar (or substitute champagne vinegar), salt and pepper to taste
1 Tbs. crushed garlic

Preparation:
1) Toss all of the above listed ingredients in a bowl with cane vinaigrette. Salt and pepper to taste.
2) Place salad at 12 O'clock on the plate. Slice rack of venison into 1 inch pieces. Place slices in front of and leaning on salad like a half-moon.
3) Drizzle reduction sauce over the top of the venison and serve.

Speckled Belly Goose Gumbo

Yields 8 entree size portions or 12 appetizer portions

Equipment:
cutting board
French knife and steel
heavy gauge soup pot $2^{1}/_{2}$ gal. or larger
wooden spoon

Roux:
$^{3}/_{4}$ cup vegetable oil
1 cup sifted flour ($^{1}/_{4}$ used to sear goose)

Mirepoix:
1 medium bunch celery cleaned and diced
4 large or 5 small onions, diced
4 green or red diced bell peppers
2 Tbs. minced garlic

Seasoning:
1 tsp. cayenne or 5 fresh diced cayenne peppers
1 pinch oregano, dry
1 pinch basil, dry
1 pinch thyme, dry
4 bay leaves
salt and black pepper to taste
1 Tbs. file powder
2 quart cold water or stock

Meat:
1 skinless speckled belly goose (You may substitute duck or chicken)
$1^{1}/_{2}$ pound andouille or any other smoked sausage (use alligator sausage when available)

Method:
1) Place the oil in a dry pot, over high heat. Heat oil to smoking point, about 5 minutes.
2) While oil is heating, cut the goose into quarters. Season heavily with salt and pepper, dust with flour. Shake off excess.
3) Sear meat in hot oil until golden brown, 1 minute on first side. Turn and sear 2 minutes on second side and remove from heat. Set aside.
4) Let oil return to smoking point again. Slowly add sifted flour, stirring constantly, until the mixture is the color of chocolate, about 3 to 5 minutes. Scraping side and bottom of pot while constantly stirring is the key to a good roux. Be careful not to burn it, because if you do, you will need to start over.
5) When roux has reached the desired color, add onions. Cook for one minute. Add celery. Cook for 30 seconds. Add bell peppers, scraping bottom of pot. Cook 1 minute.
6) Add garlic, then all remaining seasoning except file powder. Add a touch of salt and black pepper.
7) Slowly add water or stock, constantly stirring.
8) Add seared goose and sausage. Bring to a boil, stirring constantly and simmer $3^{1}/_{2}$ hours (if using chicken, cook $2^{1}/_{2}$ hours). Skim off excess fat. When meat falls off all bones, remove from pot.
9) Bring back to a boil, stir in file. Stir vigorously to avoid clumping until file is dissolved
10) Add salt and pepper to taste. Finish with Louisiana style hot sauce of your choice and taste. Adjust seasonings if necessary. Do not be afraid to spice it up! Serve over cooked white rice, and garnish with a chiffonade of green onions.

Fig Tart

Filling Ingredients:
2 lb. fresh figs, stems off
2 Tbs. sugar
$^{1}/_{4}$ cup sugar
$^{1}/_{4}$ cup molasses
$^{1}/_{4}$ cup lemon juice
$^{1}/_{2}$ cup Madeira wine

Pie Dough Ingredients:
$4^{1}/_{4}$ cups flour
1 lb. butter, diced into $^{1}/_{8}$" cubes
$^{1}/_{4}$ cup ice water
$^{1}/_{3}$ cup toasted pecans
1 tsp. cinnamon
1 Tbs. sugar

Garnish:
4 oz. chopped white chocolate

Preparation:
1) Over low heat cook all the filling ingredients until it becomes the consistency of jam, about 40 minutes. Remove from heat. (You could substitute with 1 pint fig preserves.)
2) Grind the pecans with flour in a food processor. Add cinnamon and sugar. Work in the butter by hand until incorporated. Work in ice water and work into balls and let rest.
3) Cut the dough in half and roll out on a floured surface. Roll the dough out to be $^{1}/_{4}$ inch thick. Work it into your deep-dish pan and leave an inch lip over the top to roll the edge.
4) Fill the tart shell with cold fig mixture and crimp the excess dough around the top. Add chopped white chocolate.
5) Bake at 350° F for 20 to 25 minutes or until done. Let rest before cutting. Top with vanilla ice cream and serve.

December

Arnaud's Restaurant

Since 1918, the legendary Arnaud's Restaurant has been serving elegant classic Creole cuisine with a menu that features world-famous originals like Shrimp Arnaud, Oysters Bienville, Trout Meuniere and Filet Mignon Charlemond at lunch, dinner, or their festive jazz brunch. Archie and Jane Casbarian and Chef Michel Clavelin offer superb food and impeccable service in a French Quarter landmark with the glow of crystal chandeliers reflected in leaded glass windows. There's a cigar bar, live jazz nightly in the Richelieu Room and the Germaine Wells Mardi Gras Museum where Arnaud's guests are treated to displays of carnival gowns and costumes, memorabilia and vintage photographs.

Fresh Salmon Tartare Canapés
Serves 8

Ingredients:
8 oz. very fresh salmon, cleaned thoroughly of bones and skin, finely chopped by hand
1/2 oz. small capers, finely chopped
one egg yolk
1/2 oz. shallots, finely diced
1 tsp. chives, finely diced
juice of 1/2 lemon
one drop of Tabasco
salt and pepper to taste
16 quail eggs, hard-boiled and peeled

Menu

Champagne
Salmon Tartare Canapés *
Miniature Oyster Newburg Bouchées

White Burgundy
La Chair de Crabes au Gratin *

Red Bordeaux
Le Coeur de Filet de Boeuf au Poivre *
Les Pommes de Terre Cocotte
Les Champignons Persilles
La Salade de Saison

Port
Les Fromages Assortis

Le Soufflé Glace Grand Marnier
Flaming Café Brûlot

menu by Arnaud's Restaurant

Method of Preparation:
1. Mix all of the ingredients except the quail eggs gently together in a wooden bowl.
2. Cut quail eggs in half and spoon the salmon tartare on top of each.

Crabmeat au Gratin
Serves 8

Ingredients:
2 oz. unsalted butter
2 lb. jumbo lump crab meat
4 oz. chopped shallots
4 oz. dry white vermouth
8 oz. beurre blanc sauce
8 oz. Hollandaise sauce
4 oz. freshly grated parmesan cheese

Preparation:
1. Sauté shallots in unsalted butter over medium heat until transparent.
2. Add crab meat, tossing lightly to preserve the lumps.
3. Add Vermouth, stirring gently and cook for 2 minutes over medium heat.
4. Remove from heat and gently add beurre blanc to crab meat mixture.
5. Place mixture in eight ramekins.
6. Top each with 1 oz of Hollandaise Sauce and 1/2 oz of parmesan cheese.
7. Place under the broiler until golden.

White Butter Sauce (Beurre Blanc)
Yields 2 cups

1/8 cup chopped shallots
1/4 teaspoon coarse white pepper
1 1/2 cups dry white wine
1/4 cup heavy cream
1/2 cup (1 stick) butter, very cold
salt

Combine the shallots, white pepper, and wine in a pot. Bring to a boil over high heat, then reduce the heat and simmer until the liquid has almost evaporated. Add the cream and reduce to one-third volume. Remove from the heat and add the butter, small amounts at a time, whipping with a whisk until the butter is completely mixed with the cream. (The sauce will separate if this is done over heat.)
Season to taste with salt.

Hollandaise Sauce
Yields about 2 cups

While among the best-known French sauces, hollandaise is one of the least agreed-upon in terms of technique. Here is Arnaud's method, showcased so elegantly over egg dishes at brunch.

6 egg yolks
2 cups (4 sticks) butter, melted
Salt and white pepper
Cayenne pepper
1 Tbs. lemon juice

Combine the egg yolks and 1 1/2 Tbs. water in the top of a double boiler and whip with a wire whisk over hot (but not boiling) water until fluffy. Slowly add the butter, whipping continuously until it blends and the sauce begins to thicken. Add salt, white pepper, and cayenne to taste, then whisk in the lemon juice.
    * Do not overheat the egg yolks, they will scramble.

Filet au Poivre
Serves 8

Ingredients:
8 tenderloin filet (8 oz.) center cut
4 oz. fresh crushed black peppercorns
salt to taste
5 oz. cognac
8 oz. veal stock
4 oz. whipping cream (32%)
2 oz. plugras butter
3 oz. clarified butter
8 each parsley sprigs

Method of Preparation:
1. Gently press cracked peppercorns to taste on both sides of each filet with the flat side of a mallet or chopper and add salt to taste.
2. Heat clarified butter in a large sauté pan over medium heat until medium hot.
3. Add meat and cook slowly for approximately 6 minutes on each side.
4. Add cognac and ignite, either by tilting the hot pan over a stove-top flame or lighting it carefully with a long match.
5. When the flames have burned out, remove the meat from the pan and place it in a 120° (oven until ready for use.
6. Add the veal stock and cream to the pan and reduce the sauce over medium heat until it reaches a creamy consistency.
7. Add the Plugras butter to the sauce, rotating the pan constantly until a creamy consistency is reached.
8. Place each filet on a dinner plate, cover with the sauce and garnish with a parsley sprig.

Sources

Menu Cards and Place Cards (p.11, 27, 31, 34, 47, 51, inside front cover)
Elizabeth Swanson
Swanson Vineyards
1000 Oakville Cross Road
Post Office Box 148
Oakville, CA 94562

Glass Flowers and Glass Flower Candleholders, Wine Goblets (p. 12 - 15) **and Glass Leaves** (p. 39) **and Glass Fish** (p. 27)
Jean Blair
New Orleans School of Glass Works & Printmaking Studio
727 Magazine Street
New Orleans, LA 70130
tel: (504) 529-7277 or (504) 529-7279
fax: (504) 539-5417
e-mail: glasswo@wave.tcs.tulane.edu

Flower Pads and Pens (p.20, 22)
New Orleans Botanical Garden Shop
1 Palm Drive
New Orleans, LA 70124
tel: (504) 483-9488

Chinese Cartons, Cards and Cubes (p. 24, 26, 38)
The Container Store
2000 Valwood Drive
Dallas, TX 75234
tel: (800) 733-3532

Torcheres (p. 28, 31)
Pier One Imports
1-800-447-4371

Linen Napkins and Cocktail Napkins (p. 49 - 51)
Orient Expressed
3905 Magazine Street
New Orleans, LA 70115
tel: (504) 899-3060

Paper and Seals (p. 45)
Scriptura
5423 Magazine Street
New Orleans, LA 70115
tel: (504) 897-1555

Stars, Swirls (and more) **Rubber Stamps and Ink Pads**
Ballard Designs
1670 De Floor Avenue
Atlanta, GA 30318-7528
tel: (800) 367-2775

Palm Trees, Hearts, Fish (and more) **Mylar Place Cards** (p. 24)
Betty Hunley Designs
6057 Magazine Street
New Orleans LA 70118
tel: (504) 895-2870

The Restaurants

Antoine's Restaurant
713 Saint Louis Street
New Orleans, LA 70130
Reservations: (504) 581-4422
Proprietor: Bernard R. Guste
Cookbook: *Antoine's Cookbook* (can be ordered from Antoine's Restaurant and from bookstores)
Website: www.antoines.com
E-mail: info@antoines.com

Arnaud's
813 Bienville Street
New Orleans, LA 70112
Reservations: (504) 523-5433
Proprietors: Jane and Archie Casbarian
Cookbook: *Arnaud's Cookbook* (order from Arnaud's Restaurant)
Website: www@arnauds.com

Bacco
310 Chartres Street
New Orleans, LA 70130
Reservations (504) 522-2426
Proprietor: Ralph Brennan
Website: www.bacco.com

Bella Luna
914 North Peters Street
New Orleans, LA 70116
Reservations: (504) 529-1583
Proprietors: Horst and Karen Pfeifer
Cookbook: Included in *Great Chefs - the Louisiana New Garde* (order from: Great Chefs Publishing, P. O. Box 56757, New Orleans, La 70156
Website::www.neworleans.net/fdpagers/bellalunarev.html

Brennan's Restaurant
417 Royal Street
New Orleans, LA 70130
Reservations (504) 525-9711
Proprietors: Pip, Jimmy and Ted Brennan
Cookbook: *Breakfast at Brennan's and Dinner Too* (order by calling 504-525-9713)
Website: www.brennansneworleans,com

Commander's Palace
1403 Washington Avenue
New Orleans, LA 70130
Reservations: (504) 899-8221
Proprietors: Ella, Dick, Dottie, and John Brennan
Cookbook: *The Commander's Palace New Orleans Cookbook* (order from 504-899-9591)
Website: www.commanderspalace.com

Dooky Chase Restaurant
2301 Orleans Avenue
New Orleans, LA 70119
Reservations (504) 821-0600
Proprietors: Edgar and Leah Chase
Cookbook: *The Dooky Chase Cookbook* (order from Pelican Publishing, Gretna, LA.)

Galatoire's
209 Bourbon Street
New Orleans, LA 70130
Reservations (504) 525-2021
Proprietors: Shareholders of Galatoire's

Joel's Grand Cuisine
503 North New Hampshire Street
Covington, LA 70433
Reservations: (504) 892-8504 or (800) 335-8994. Proprietor: Joel Dondis
Website: www.joels.com

Mr. B's Bistro
201 Royal Street
New Orleans, LA 70130
Reservations (504) 523-2078
Proprietor: Cindy Brennan
Website: www.mrbsbistro.com

Catalogue

"Celebration" Table Decor has been custom designed by Bev Church with metal sculptors, Luis Colmenares and Julia Yerkov. Each item is a hand crafted and unique artwork to enhance your special tables. The attached glass vials will hold your favorite blooms to create a dramatic "tablescape" with minimum effort!

1.

2.

3.

4.

5A.

5B.

Entertaining Celebrations - *Celebrate Each Month with Pizzazz!*
by Beverly Reese Church...Item #A ....$ 28.

Celebration Gift Certificate (In special presentation wrapping)
In the amount you specify...Item #B ....minimum $ 50.

1. **Large Celebration Centerpiece** (With eight lg. vials)
Approx 38" high (p. 49)...Item #1....................$240.

2. **Large Banana Tree Centerpiece** (Comes with flower vial)
Banana Tree, approx 40" high (p. 35)...Item #2 ....$240.

3. **Large Metal Palm Tree Centerpiece**
Approx 33" high. (see p. 32)...Item #3 ....$240.

4. **Single Celebration Vase** (With one lg. flower vial)
Approx 8" (see p. 48, 49)...Item #4 ....$ 22.
1 small vial...Item #4A ....$ 4.
1 large vial...Item #4B ....$ 5.

5. **Small Metal Palm Tree Flower Holders** (With one sm. vial)
About 6" high (see p. 35)...Item #5A ....$ 22.
Also available as Banana Tree design...Item #5B.........$ 22.

Celebration Chair Back Bouquet (Comes with one lg. vial)
(see p. 48, 49, 50)...Item #6..$ 28.

Handpainted Napkin/Scarf (about 20" square-washable) by Ray Cole
(shown wrapping a box p. 5)...Item #7..........................$ 25.

Handpainted "Fish" or "Leaf" Place Mats (washable) by Ray Cole
Fish design, approx 21" (p. 5)...Item #8A......................$ 40.
Leaf design, approx 21" ...Item #8B..............................$ 40.

Chef's Aprons, in 100% cotton (p. 5)
1 apron...Item #9A ....$ 6.
1 dozen aprons...Item #9B ....$ 70.

Waist Aprons, 100% cotton (p.20)
1 apron...Item #10A ....$ 6.
1 dozen aprons...Item #10B...$ 70.

Antique Gold Painted Leaves
(p. 48, 50)
1 large bunch...Item #11. ....$ 13.

Topiary Forms (p. 50, 51, 68)
Single Ball, 18" high...Item #12A................................$ 10.
Double Ball, 21" high...Item #12B ....$ 11.
Cone Shaped, 21" high...Item #12C.............................$ 11.

Oasis, pre-formed into shapes
2 rings, 10" (p. 32, 34)...Item #13A ....$ 21.
1 heart, 12" (p. 8, 9, 58)...Item #13B..........................$ 15.

White Boxes
1 - 6"x6"x4" (p.35, 48, 49, 50, 51, 64)...Item #14A ......$ 1.25
1 - 4"x4"x4" (p. 5, 26)...Item #14B................................$ 0.80

Prices may be subject to change.

Order Form

Entertaining Celebrations
5500 Prytania Street, Box 402
New Orleans, LA 70115

Your name and address:

_____
_____
_____

How did you hear of Entertaining Celebrations?
_____

Would you like to receive a newsletter? _____

If the address at left is a P.O. Box or you have a different "ship to" address, please give us your shipping address below. (No P. O. boxes please.)

Your shipping street address:

_____
_____
_____

Telephone (day)   (   ) _____-_____
Telephone (evening) (   ) _____-_____

Don't forget about Gift Certificates!

Books will be shipped within seven working days. For other items, please allow 6 - 8 weeks delivery.

Item #	Quantity	Item Description	Size (if applicable)	Price Per Item	Total Price

Gift 1   To: Name _____   Recipient's Telephone (   ) _____-_____
                Address _____   Gift Message _____
                             _____   (please print) _____

Item #

Gift 2   To: Name _____   Recipient's Telephone (   ) _____-_____
                Address _____   Gift Message _____
                             _____   (please print) _____

Item #

Payment Method

Enclose your personal check or money order, or enter your Visa or Mastercard information below

☐ Check   ☐ Visa
☐ Money Order   ☐ MasterCard

Card Account Number

☐☐☐☐☐☐☐☐☐☐☐☐☐☐☐☐

Expiration Date
☐☐ - ☐☐

_____
Signature of Authorized Buyer

Check out
www.beverlychurch.com,
the source for easy,
elegant and affordable
entertaining! E-mail your
orders and questions to
beverlychurch@hotmail.com

Merchandise Total ☐
Add delivery charges per address ☐
La. residents please add sales tax ☐
Total ☐

Thank you for your order!

From:

_____

_____

_____

Entertaining Celebrations
Attention: Mail Order
5500 Prytania Street
Box 402
New Orleans, Louisiana 70115

— Please fold closed on dotted lines and seal...

Your Notes and Ideas

Index of Projects

* Page numbers in black are for instructions; numbers in red are photographs and illustrations.

Index of Recipes

Acknowledgements

Entertaining Celebrations - Celebrate Each Month With Pizzazz! has been a joy to create because of all the talented professionals and friends who have helped me put this project together. Tina Freeman's uncanny ability to capture each setting with exquisite lighting and her creative vision brought the color and excitement of each month "to life." Often, we had very long days and I appreciate her efforts, friendship and pure talent!

Sallye Irvine is an exceptional writer that I've gotten to know well over the past two years. She has been able to translate my thoughts into flowing text with a "spark" and "vigor" that we both share. Her expertise and knowledge have been priceless.

Elizabeth Pipes Swanson, my oldest and dearest friend created the wonderful, whimsical watercolor paintings that you see as menu cards throughout the book. The joy and talent she possesses are a gift that I will always be grateful she has shared with all of us. You'll be able to buy her menu cards, place cards, note paper, and specialty items for the first time!

The most prestigious New Orleans restaurants, their owners, chefs and proprietors have put together menus, recipes and wine suggestions for each month. New Orleans is known world wide for our cuisine, and many of these recipes were created especially for *Entertaining Celebrations*. Many, many thanks to the restaurants: Antoine's, Arnaud's, Bacco, Bella Luna, Brennan's, Commander's Palace, Dooky Chase, Galatoire's, Joel's Grand Cuisine, Mike's on the Avenue, and Mr. B's Bistro.

Kristin O'Loughlin has designed this book with a distinctive and creative flair and her dedicated work has been appreciated and invaluable.

Special thanks go to Bill Bell, Trevor Sprague and the great staff at Upton Printing and to Sue Strachan, my dear friend who offered editing advice.

Thanks also go out to my friends who allowed me to use their beautiful homes and country houses as locations for my monthly parties.

And last, but not least, thanks to God, who continually watches over me, and to my family, who gives me unconditional love and support in all of my endeavors.

And to the many others who have helped me with this book in countless ways, I want to thank you all warmly...

Adams and Reese, Afton Villa Plantation, Kay Bailey, John D. Baumhauer, Vicky Bayley, Ellen and Ted Brennan, Lally Brennan, Linda Reese Bjork, Rob Bjork, Heidi Bjork, Gretchen Bjork, Foster Blair, Jeannie Blair, Cindy Brennan, Ralph and Susan Brennan, Andy and Kellie Brott, Leah Chase, Chris and Joan Church, C.J. and Lauren Church, Ray Cole, Tommy and Dathel Coleman, Luis Colmenares, Isabelle Colmenares, Zoe Colmenares, Angus Cooper, Rob Couhig, Joel Dondis, Patrick Dunne, Alexis Swanson Farrer, Judith Feagin, Mike Fennelly, Justin Frey, David Gooch, Terri Havens, Betty Hunley, Susan and Doug Johnson, Minnie Hinton, Ashley Houk, Sallye and George Irvine, Ivy Jones, Kay and Bobby Kerrigan, Ashley Kostmayer, Mathilde and Prieur Leary, Lucullus Antiques, Jimmy Maxwell, Missy McLellan, Michelle McRaney, Kerry Moody, Ainsley and Miles Mumford, Marianne and Alan Mumford, Charlee Marshall, Marguerite Nash, The New Orleans Botanical Garden, Mike Owen, Christopher Peters, Karen and Horst Pfeiffer, Susan and Bill Prentiss, Thomas Ford Reese, Carol Reese, Byrne Reese, Bonnie Reese, Beverly Hess Reese, Pixie and Jimmy Reiss, Crutcher Reiss, Melvin Rodrigue, César Rodriguez, Mike Roussel, Jamie Shannon, Paul Soniat, Sue Strachan, Clarke Swanson, Zoubir Tabout, Mr. and Mrs. Morrell Trimble, Lynne and Hunter White, Charles Willoughby, Olivia Woollam and Julia Yerkov.

...Beverly Reese Church